Wisdom

By DANIEL BERRIGAN

Prose

The Bride: Essays in the Church
The Bow in the Clouds
Consequences, Truth and
Love, Love at the End
They Call Us Dead Men
Night Flight to Hanoi
No Bars to Manhood
The Dark Night of Resistance
America Is Hard to Find
The Geography of Faith (with Robert Coles)
Absurd Convictions, Modest Hopes (with Lee Lockwood)
Jesus Christ
Lights On in the House of the Dead
The Raft Is Not the Shore (with Thich Nhat Hahn)
A Book of Parables
Uncommon Prayer: A Book of Psalms
Beside the Sea of Glass: The Song of the Lamb
The Words Our Savior Taught Us
The Discipline of the Mountain
We Die before We Live
Portraits: Of Those I Love
Ten Commandments for the Long Haul
Nightmare of God
Steadfastness of the Saints
The Mission
To Live in Peace: Autobiography
A Berrigan Reader
Stations (with Margaret Parker)
Sorrow Built a Bridge
Wheron to Stand (Acts of the Apostles)
Minor Prophets, Major Themes
Isaiah: Spirit of Courage, Gift of Tears
Ezekiel: Vision in the Dust
Jeremiah: The World, the Wound of God
Daniel: Under the Siege of the Divine
Job: And Death No Dominion
Wisdom: The Feminine Face of God

Poetry

Time without Number
Encounters
The World for Wedding Ring
No One Walks Waters
False Gods, Real Men
Trial Poems (with Tom Lewis)
Prison Poems
Selected & New Poems
May All Creatures Live
Block Island
Jubilee
Tulips in the Prison Yard
Homage (to G. M. Hopkins)
And the Risen Bread

Drama

The Trial of the Catonsville Nine

Wisdom

THE FEMININE FACE OF GOD

DANIEL BERRIGAN

ART *by* ROBERT MCGOVERN

SHEED & WARD
Franklin, Wisconsin
Chicago

2001

Sheed & Ward
7373 South Lovers Lane Road
Franklin, Wisconsin 53132
1-800-266-5564

Printed in the United States of America
"Dialectic" by R. S. Thomas is from *Collected Poems* by R. S. Thomas, JM Dent, Publisher.
Cover and interior design: Madonna Gauding

Library of Congress Cataloging-in-Publication Data

Berrigan, Daniel.
  Wisdom: the feminine face of God / Daniel Berrigan; with art by Robert McGovern.
        p.cm.
    ISBN 1-58051-100-7
        1. Bible. O.T. Apocrypha. Wisdom of Solomon—Commentaries.
2. Wisdom (Biblical personification) 3. Femininity of God. I. Title.

BS1755.53 .B47 2001
229'.3077—dc21

2001049571

1 2 3 4 5 / 04 03 02 01

To Sister Anne Montgomery, R.S.C.J.
Hero
from Ploughshares Prisons
to embattled Hebron

Contents

Foreword

In the summer of 1971, between my sophomore and junior years in high school, I came across a thin, paperback book in a drugstore at the Delaware Plaza in Delmar, New York, my hometown. It was compiled by David Kirk of the Emmaus community in Harlem and it was entitled *Quotations from Chairman Jesus*. The allusion to Mao was lost on me, but the title intrigued me nonetheless, and so did the book as I thumbed through the pages. It contained passages from Scripture set off by section titles such as "The Way of the Cross: Shalom" and "The Revolutionary Ethic of Jesus Compared to the Ordinary Guidelines for Society." The last part consisted of quotations from early Church figures, Gregory of Nyssa, Basil of Caesaria, John Chrysostom, among others, all gathered under the heading "Fathers of the Revolution." I bought the book, took it home, and started reading it that afternoon, beginning with the foreword, which included the following *credo*:

> I can only tell you what I believe. I believe
> > I cannot be saved by foreign policies
> > I cannot be saved by sexual revolutions
> > I cannot be saved by the gross national product
> > I cannot be saved by nuclear deterrents,
> > I cannot be saved by aldermen, priests, artists,
> > > plumbers, city planners, social engineers,
> > > nor by the Vatican, nor by the World Buddhist
> > > > Association
> > > nor by Hitler nor by Joan of Arc
> > > nor by angels and archangels nor by powers
> > > and dominations.
> I can be saved only by Jesus Christ.

This string of renunciations won my immediate approval, except the one about sexual revolutions (which would have spoiled some indefinite but deeply cherished plans for the near or distant future). But what was most striking about this passage was the profession of faith. Having attended public schools my whole life and survived several years of C.C.D., it had never occurred to me that an interesting alternative to the many salvations bought and sold on the cultural market of the early seventies could be found in Jesus Christ.

At supper that night, I told everyone at the table about the book, and mentioned as well the author of the foreword. My father, a World War II veteran who had scorn for everything associated with "the counter-culture," immediately muttered some expletive. My sister laughed. My mother scolded my father. And my brother-in-law, realizing that I knew nothing about the foreword's author, proceeded to explain to me who this Daniel Berrigan was: priest, poet, anti-war activist, draft-file burner, convicted felon, fugitive from the law, and for the past year or so, an inmate at Danbury Federal Penitentiary. My interest was definitely piqued. How is it, I wondered, that such a life could be lived by someone who is not embarrassed to declare, in print no less, "I can only be saved by Jesus Christ"?

Thirty years later, the answer to that question has been made much clearer to me, thanks in large part to the homilies Daniel Berrigan has preached, the retreats he has led, the protests he has undertaken, the prison sentences he has served (during which he continues to minister "on the inside"), and the books he has written—including this book, which shows that this kind of life is the fruit of Wisdom.

The upper case is important here: Wisdom. For the Book of Wisdom does not extol some generic sense of wisdom, nor the various wisdoms of the world. It extols the Wisdom by which all Creation was created, which was set forth in the Law and the prophets, and which will restore us to peace with God and one another, if only we live in accord with Her counsel. Given his longstanding view on salvation, Daniel believes that we are made capable of living by Wisdom in and through the life, death, and resurrection of Jesus Christ. This is in keeping with an unmistakable theological tradition extending from Origen to Augustine to Aquinas to John Paul II (to name a few), which holds, to put it bluntly, that Jesus Christ is Wisdom.

In the meditations that follow, it is this unmistakably orthodox understanding of Wisdom which is brought into conversation with themes that are readily associated with Daniel's poetic pen: the imperatives of peace and justice, the encroachments of the imperium, the infidelities of religious establishment, the costs of true discipleship. These themes are usually labeled "prophetic" and then attached to prophetic types, Catholic Workers, Plowshares Activists, and others of the radical Christian Left whose voices all too often get relegated, sometimes with their own consent, to the margins of the Church's life and work. Daniel's reflections resist such marginalization. The reasoning is disarmingly simple: if "Wisdom is a spirit friendly to humanity" (Wisdom 1:6), and if Jesus embodies the fullness of Wisdom, then following Jesus' teaching and example on peacemaking and the works of mercy in a literal way places us not at the margins of the Church but at the center. Indeed, when Wisdom is defined in this traditional, christological manner, conventional conceptions of center and margin are re-configured such that this kind of life is affirmed on the strongest theological grounds conceivable, on the grounds that it is revealed by God as the kind of life for which all human beings were created and in which they can truly flourish. Thus at one point, Daniel notes that the Gift of Wisdom "enables us to comport ourselves as humans." But he goes on from here to add, "and this against the odds of an inhuman time," thus acknowledging that comporting ourselves as humans entails denouncing inhumanity wherever it occurs, on battlefields and death rows, in fields and factories, in torture chambers and abortion clinics. This is an important acknowledgment, for while inhumanity may be widely justified in the name of "national security," "law and order," "the free market," "choice," or whatever ideology prevails in a given society, this does not mean that those who prophetically denounce it should be written off as marginal. It may well mean the opposite: that the given society should be viewed as marginal to the purposes of God. Or to put it in other words, the predominant wisdom of a given society may not be wisdom at all, but a simulacrum of wisdom, indeed foolishness. And Christians should not be surprised that this often turns out to be the case, for the Wisdom of which we speak "is not a wisdom of this age, nor of the rulers of this age, who are headed for destruction. No, what we utter is God's wisdom: a mysterious, a hidden wisdom" (see 1 Corinthians 2: 6–7).

Daniel's commentary on the Book of Wisdom can be located within a theological tradition dedicated to articulating what has been called "the Radical Christianity of the Gospel." The phrase comes from the subtitle of *Your Ways Are Not My Ways,* by John J. Hugo, a priest-mentor of Dorothy Day. Half a century ago, theologians accused Hugo, and by association Day, of falling into the error of Jansenism (for which Hugo was at one point silenced). Theologians of this generation echo these criticisms when they accuse the theological heirs of Hugo and Day of being "sectarian" or "against culture." Taken together, the gist of the criticism is that proponents of radical Christianity deny the fundamental goodness of human nature, regard society and culture as evil, and call upon Christians to withdraw into their own enclave. Although these criticisms have become standard fare among Catholic and Protestant theologians, they are ultimately groundless, and Daniel's reflections help us to see why.

For one thing, nowhere in these pages is it suggested that nature must be spurned as evil. On the contrary, Daniel finds in the Book of Wisdom what he calls "radiant theology of grace," wherein Wisdom is suffused throughout all creation. This vision does not betray a Jansenist denigration of nature. It is more aptly associated with the *nouvelle théologie* of Henri de Lubac, whose work deeply influenced Daniel when he was a Jesuit scholastic in France during the fifties. For de Lubac, nature is fundamentally good, but its goodness leaves us thirsting for the greater good of supernatural life with Christ and in the Church. Or again, nowhere in these pages is it stated that Christians should withdraw from society. Rather, Daniel finds that at the heart of Wisdom is the call for justice and that justice requires Christians to attend to the needs of those whom society has forgotten. This is not a sectarian movement away from society but *toward* society, in the direction indicated by the Second Vatican Council in its Pastoral Constitution of the Church in the Modern World, that is, toward those who are poor or in any way afflicted, whose joys, hopes, griefs, and anxieties are to be taken on by the followers of Christ (see *Gaudium et Spes*, n. 1). Daniel acquired this pastoral impulse well before the Council, once again, during his early years in France, under the influence of fellow Jesuit Henri Perrin, a leader in the Worker-Priest Movement. Or to take another example, nothing in these pages indicates a wholesale rejection of culture. Rather, Daniel finds the Book of Wisdom calling us to judge each culture, and each aspect of each culture, according to the standards of Divine Wisdom revealed in the Law and in Christ and to embrace or reject it accordingly. Here, too, we see evidence of Daniel's Jesuit formation. In good Ignatian fashion, we are called to see God in all things: at the same time, we are also called, in equally Ignatian fashion, to make sure that it is God whom we see and not some idol of our own making. In this understanding , the relationship between Divine Wisdom and human wisdom is complex. It defies simple formulation. Whether or not a particular cultural form or practice can be embraced by Christians is a matter that requires prayer, meditation on Scripture, critical reflection, and judgment: in a word, discernment. Granted, there will be times when the discernment calls for opposition, but this is nothing more than what Pope John Paul II calls for in the encyclical *Evangelium Vitae* (nn. 73–74) when it comes to evil practices in a culture of death.

So these reflections on the Book of Wisdom are guided by a theology that is at once radical and orthodox, and thus thoroughly compelling. As a theologian by trade, I could elaborate on the themes found in Daniel's commentary that resonate with the leading emphases of several important theologians and theological movements that have appeared in recent years: with the scriptural interpretation offered by Walter Brueggeman and Walter Wink: with the account of Christian peacemaking articulated by John Howard Yoder and Gerhardt Lohfink: with the christologically shaped moral theology developed by Servais Pinckaers and Romanus Cessario: with the view of the modern state put forth by Alasdair MacIntyre and Anthony Giddens: with the vision of the Church presented by Michael Budde and Phil Kenneson: with the narrative theology formulated by George Lindbeck and Stanley Hauerwas: and with the critique of secular social theory in favor of a theologically grounded social theory advanced by John Milbank, Catherine Pickstock, and others associated with the movement dubbed Radical Orthodoxy. But there is a danger in drawing out and lingering over these connections—not that the connections are not there. They are—but demonstrating that they are there in the elaborate manner of professional theologians might give the impression that this book is designed to make its mark in theological circles. This is not the case. This book, while certainly theologically informed, is free of the typical trappings of professional theology: subtle and complicated conceptual analyses, detailed cross-references, lengthy footnotes, neologisms, and so on. There is, I believe, a wisdom to this, for one of the debilitating effects of professional theology is that it keeps its practitioners in the stacks and thus off the streets, whereas Daniel wants us theologians to hit the streets.

I recently received a note from Daniel along with a poem entitled "Prison, 2001." It was written for his brother Phillip on the occasion of his being sentenced, along with three others, to another year in prison in Portland, Maine. At one point, the poem reads:

> O my brother, ten like your soul, only ten,
> and the times are redeemed.
> You, Susan, Greg, Steven—God keeps count,
> wills the total—
>
> like a priest's cup passed, full, unfailing,
> breathing sacrament.

As I read, the poem made its point, hit the bull's-eye, put the question to its reader: When are the theologians going to add themselves to the ten? When are they going to help fill this blessed and costly cup? When are *you*? Daniel's answer would echo the words of that inmate of the *imperium* whom the Church calls apostle and saint: "Now is the acceptable time. Now is the day of salvation" (2 Corinthians 6:2). I can hear him chanting it now, urging us, as he has for the better part of four decades, to stand up at a faculty meeting and be heard, or better yet, to sit down at the entry of a ROTC building and be heard.

On May 9, 2001, Daniel celebrated his eightieth birthday. When people who came of age during the sixties hear about Daniel turning eighty, they oftentimes recall Catonsville and express astonishment that he's still getting arrested. At times, it is with a wistful tone, signifying regret perhaps over the loss of the conviction of their youth: at other times, with a tone of disdain, as if to suggest that someone his age should have outgrown such antics long ago. This, I suppose, is how many people view the life Daniel has lived: in some sense admirable, but ultimately, immature and rather foolish. But on the weekend before his birthday, hundreds of Daniel's family, friends, and co-workers gathered in New York to mark his life as well lived. The gathering did not represent a majority of the nation, nor of the Church, nor even of his own community. But "the wise," Aquinas assures us, rarely constitute the preponderance of a populace, nor is Wisdom ever determined by popular vote. Wisdom has to do with living a certain kind of life, not unlike the kind of life Daniel has lived: praying, visiting the sick, giving retreats, getting arrested and sent to prison, and of course, all the while, writing.

Writing: spending hours each morning meditating on sacred Scripture, reading commentaries and theologies, pondering and pacing and putting words on a page, then casting them about, like seeds from the hand of the generous Sower, some of which fall on hard ground or rocky or thorny ground, and some which fall on fertile ground. These seeds which are words, these seeds of the Word, can end up anywhere, in the most unlikely of places, even on a bookrack in a drugstore at the Delaware Plaza in Delmar, New York, where half-bored, half-curious teenagers might glance at them and realize, in a way for the first time, that they can be saved only by Jesus Christ, where they might come away intrigued enough to learn what this salvation looks like when lived.

To the wise of this world, living one's life in accord with the simple credo, "I can be saved only by Jesus Christ," writing about it, acting on it, may seem like foolishness. But, as Jesus said, referring to the ministry of John the Baptist (see Matthew 11:19), "Time will prove where Wisdom lies."

Michael J. Baxter, C.S.C.
University of Notre Dame
June 24, 2001
Feast of the Birth of John the Baptist

Preface

I take literally the statement in the gospel of John that God loves the world.
I believe that the world was created and approved by love, and that, inso-
far as it is redeemable, it can be redeemed only by love.

I believe that divine love, incarnate and indwelling in the world, summons the world always toward wholeness, which ultimately is reconciliation
and atonement with God.

(*Another Turn of the Crank,* Wendell Berry)

✦　✦　✦

Let us venture an analogy with our book of Wisdom.

Let us even suppose something unlikely.

In this tangled jungle known as American culture, the hothouse of
every sweet and seductive *florum,* an *imperium* of desire and appetite, a
fierce threshing ground of the human, an induction center in the art and
practice of amnesia—and always and everywhere violence, violence—in
this unlikely place and time, there exists a community of believers.

That in itself is astonishing, since the culture is a primary, massive,
militarized, antihuman disbeliever.

Such effrontery! Believers? A community of such? The notion is an offense. The culture believes in—itself. In what strikes the fancy or appetite
of the moment, what serves self-interest or feeds concupiscent eyes or the
dogging impulse of domination. A corporate believer in whatever price
our system, if it is to stand intact, must exact of others: and so be it. (The
death of Iraqi children included, as our Sibyl of State has famously
intoned).

Indeed, to serve the good life, the word *belief* must be stretched to the
utmost, to the near absurd. The culture is a limitless appetitive seeking
after "the things which are seen." This is the game, as agreed on, and
played to the hilt.

And all this, of course, makes inevitable a fierce opposition to the faithful minority—that handful of folks who (at least in principle), are vowed
to pursue "the things which are unseen."

✦　✦　✦

It is even claimed by these latter that they see the unseen.

And what do they see that others do not see? It is strange, they hold in memory a story, of a given time and place, peopled by mysterious, holy women and men, walking this world.

A tragic story, as they tell it, and a glorious one. They see it in the mind's eye, they can name its chief provocateurs and actors, its heroes and villains. They summon some among these, saints and martyrs, to their side, to their succor—even to their joy.

And this occurs: from time to time, the believing folk judge that they require a reminding. Their story, the story that unites and keeps them going, must not fall out of the world, become frayed or old hat, or be swamped by other tales.

A real danger, this latter. Look out, the culture has other stories! It is a fiercely fermenting vat of images, a vintage of "things seen": and more, of things tasted, smelled, touched, heard in the inner ear, had by heart—longed for, bought, bargained for, stolen, possessed, owned, controlled.

✦　✦　✦

Thus these minority folk are assailed by other versions of reality than their own. Stories concerning "things seen," stories that resemble their own in this: those other histories unite fellow citizens and keep them going, keep them complaisant and in step. And most important of all, keep the system humming.

✦　✦　✦

Let us suppose then, an intrusion on things as they are. In the midst of this believing handful there exists a seer, regarded with respect and love. He is one with these believers, an embracing, welcoming spirit. And he can strike hard, this one!

He ponders the situation of his own, amid the ferocious larger scene. And in due time he sets down a reflection, a treatise of sorts. But with no heavy hand, no moral hammering away.

He knows too that a letter to the "faithful" will be of small help. Preaching to the choir!

No, he must address people, whatever their belief, across the board. On the order of say, a letter of Pope John. In effect a love letter—to the world! A *Mater et Magister*, a *Pacem in Terris*.

✦　✦　✦

That might befit, might gain a hearing. Something like this:

"Dear foolish world-at-large, salutations! Together with yourselves, I wish to celebrate the genius and urbanity and ardor which are your gifts.

"I wish also to add an 'alas.' I note something to reprove, indeed to denounce, in your behavior. I mean the misery of multitudes, together with the surfeit of appetite and grubby greed that thrive among you, the profitless rattling of weaponry, the diplomatic chicanery. Nothing of this does you honor . . ." And so on and so on. Start with love, lace the love with heartfelt instruction. Clarify what is muddy, encourage half-nascent goodness, reprove the high and mighty, defend and cherish the victims. You'll gain a hearing!

✦   ✦   ✦

The above perhaps is a plausible parallel with the book before us, our book of Wisdom.

We are told of a community of Jews, dispersed in Alexandria, the Greek capital of Egypt. There, enticements fall heavy—to assimilate, to forget.

Evidence of Greek genius is everywhere apparent: in philosophy, a theology of sorts, in drama both tragic and funny, in military prowess, eloquence, political savvy. In sum, in the fine play of high culture.

Glorious, enticing!

✦   ✦   ✦

Granted all this, celebrating this, let our "hosts" know that we believers honor a principle we see embodied in themselves: *nil humanum a me alienum*, "We Jews, like yourselves, are inimical to nothing human."

Which dictum leaves one vaguely dissatisfied: too negative! Better: we honor every evidence of goodness, art, valor, literary greatness that we see flourishing among you.

So. Let us compose a letter, addressed to Hebrews and Greeks alike. To declare publicly our love for all. To urge this sense on our community: love, embrace, "whatever is good, whatever noble." And to urge a like sense among the Greeks: "pursue, cherish whatever is good, whatever noble."

Our letter to the world will indulge a literary artifice. The purported author will be a paragon of wisdom both sacred and profane—for example, a Solomon.

✦   ✦   ✦

Inevitably, questions arise. Someone, perhaps a royal patron, has set down our book of Wisdom.

Who might this one be, what vision drives him? The question, let it be adduced, is a major ingredient of the charm of the book: it teases us, leads us along an unmarked path. So much is left to ourselves, to our ingenuity, our feel for context, our analogies of faith.

Can we then create a kind of midrash of the mind, can we stand outside the text, as well as within? Are we confident of our experience, can we judge what goes on here, summon our lives as witnesses, as though we belonged in the text—as though the text belonged to us?

✦   ✦   ✦

Another question: is the author's stance to be thought historical or prophetic? Does he accept whole cloth the stories surrounding Solomon? Does he have no quarrel with the king's historians and their writings, a *pentimento* of self-serving glory?

And what to make of the god of Solomon, that inciter of wars and alarms, no critic of royal behavior, of forced labor, grandiose architecture, standing armies, and greed for glory? Is this deity acceptable, does (s)he correspond to our own story of God, our gospel of Jesus?

Or is the book of Wisdom to be judged an extended oxymoron, a critique of inhuman power, a warning issued to believers and Greeks alike—to beware the ideology of a Solomon? Is the great king summoned to a judgment none the less dire for being implied?

And more: is Solomon here devalued, subtly derided as a type, a cliché of power gone to rot? Solomon, a symbol of the malaise endemic to imperial appetite, its violence and intrigue and cruelty—then and now?

Acknowledgments

By hook and crook, in courts and jails and classrooms, through family and friends, including my beloved Jesuit community of West 98th Street, "The Feminine Face of God" revealed itself. Extraordinary women offered me their friendship. I name in the first place my mother, Frida Fromhart. Then my sisters-in-law, Rosalie Moore, Carol Rizzo, Elizabeth McAlister, Virginia Berrigan. And many others, known to my grateful heart, who stood with me. In dark hours, but for them, I would surely have been discredited and disposed of.

Let these few words bespeak a lifetime of respect and love.

Through such friends, Hagia Sophia has shown the Feminine Face of God to me.

✦ ✦ ✦

My gratitude to artist Robert McGovern, whose acute eye has uncovered in the text of Wisdom riches hidden from most of us—including the author.

And due thanks to Michael Baxter; his introduction is judicious and generous, as always.

Salaam and shalom to Jeremy Langford, staunch friend, an editor who misses neither jot nor tittle.

Introduction

According to Catholics, Wisdom is integral to the vast biblical canvas. And one thinks gratefully, what a wise inclusion, and how poor we would be, deprived of this voice! The Church is in its debt; we borrow and borrow the splendid aphorisms, ironies, and moral instructions for our liturgies and yearlong cycle of liturgical prayers.

My reflections on the Book of Wisdom owe much to Thomas Merton; and thereby hangs a tale. Sometime in the fifties, a drawing by an artist friend arrived in Merton's mail. The gift was a simple line drawing of a mother, a child standing at center—woman and boy facing the viewer. The artist wrote that the image had grown as though spontaneously under his hand; he was uncertain as to the identity of the woman and child.

Merton was intrigued and moved. He pondered the drawing, and in time came up with an insight. (This was nothing new, this monkish clairvoyance). The woman in the drawing, he declared, was "Hagia Sophia," Hole Wisdom, and Her Child was of course Jesus.

Shortly thereafter Merton composed an ecstatic prose poem in honor of the sublime, indeed divine Feminine. The text is one of his finest, and was eventually published, together with the drawing.

Parts of this paean dovetailed nicely, I thought, with my reflections on Wisdom. I borrowed larcenously, and sections of Merton's ode to Wisdom grace my text. He would hardly have minded.

✦　✦　✦

One quickly learns, and with considerable chagrin, that in the Wisdom literature of our Bible (i.e., the present book, together with Ben Sira and Proverbs), there are no straight emotional narrative guidelines. Up and down disconcertingly, in and out, the ecstatic yields to the banal, sound instruction falls to sexism or cruelty toward children, the scribes borrow without scruple from goy sources, they scrap earlier versions of Exodus in grandiloquent favor of the tribe and its immaculate conception.

What survives the centuries and arrives in our hands is a kind of wide-ranging anthology. The texts include moral teaching, poetry, and history. They are also marked (and marred) by personal pique, classism, sexism, fear, and animosity toward slaves, little or no attribution and considerable bowing and scraping in the direction of dubious kings.

The Wisdom literature is in sum, shockingly inferior in comparison with the prophets (though in our book of Wisdom, a cap is tipped now and then in their direction). The earlier, more or less official histories of the kings also undergo a serious second look, and adjustments.

And in that task, another surprise; in Wisdom and elsewhere, Solomon's name and fame are invoked, a famous fiction. And lest we miss it, the sun king himself instructs us at length, directly, as though his pontifications were set in bold print. Quite a daring devise, in sum.

✦   ✦   ✦

It leads and lends itself to our own gospel, this book of Wisdom. Luke is enchanted by the multifarious Gift, incarnate in Jesus. He, we are told, early on "grew in wisdom," the understanding of an alert and intelligent child, on His way to brimming human fullness.

The mature Man emerged. The "Jesus Wisdom," it became evident, was unpalatable to Romans, scribes, and the temple claque, in collusion, willfully ignorant of His holiness and mission.

God turned elsewhere, Jesus thundered, turned—to "merest children," to whom was given, in a charming phrase, "mouth and wisdom."

The gift was robust; it must be to serve dire circumstances. This Jesus insists "His fate is one with the disciples." The forces that will bring Him down "will manhandle and persecute you, summoning you to prisons, bringing you to trial . . ."

(Plowshares prisoners, take note, take heart!)

✦   ✦   ✦

The text of Wisdom, it seemed to me for years, vibrates, ricochets, lays a command. In the night of drawn swords, the imperative becomes a kind of mantra: Bring Wisdom to bear!

In effect, awful events of my lifetime demand that a further step, a kind of vigorous, physical midrash be ventured.

The book of Wisdom led to the "Christ Wisdom" of Luke, then that incarnate Wisdom led to a further translation or accommodation. To action. To resistance. An attempt to illumine, in light of the text, the overbearing unwisdom, the necrophiliac antiwisdom of my culture.

The text could be seen as a kind of relief map of the times. Open and read, ponder the moral terrain, and grow wise!

Then walk and walk. Together with martyrs and persecutors, holy ones under assault, wicked rulers, the remorseful, those rightly condemned, those crowned with eternal life, idolaters and true believers, saints and charlatans—here, in this raging, ecstatic, bracing, brutal scramble—this book, its world unmasked. And our own as well.

✦   ✦   ✦

When a text is so belabored and mauled over centuries, choices as to what versions to follow become difficult. My method is outrageously unacademic. My prime source is the original French version of the Bible of Jerusalem (referred to as BJ in the text), with at times, serious reservations. The New American Standard (NAS) is helpful and thought provoking, and invites increased respect for our common resources. So a Catholic version of the same, the New American Bible (NAB), has been a staunch friend.

The Revised Standard Version (NRSV) stands elegantly in the lineage of King James—a reminder and a reproof. Magnificent, sonorous prose. Guard it well.

"The Spirit fills the universe. Be just, you rulers, and take note" (1:1–2:24)

1:1 No preliminaries here! We begin like the blast of a shofar. Great Solomon (purportedly) exhorts his fellow rulers: love justice!

The fiction is wonderfully ironic. Solomon a lover of justice?

Or his imperial cohorts across the world—or across time, today—heeding such a call?

Undoubtedly our author is well versed in the prophets of his own faith. One among the great ones, Isaiah, by strong implication took a dim view of the likes of Solomon—and this regarding the supposition on which our (suppositious) Solomon proceeds, i.e., that the likes of Solomon cherish justice.

A dim view indeed. According to the prophet, justice among the "nations" is strictly an import: it is not, cannot be, native to their soil.

Rather, justice is the heavy charge laid on the "servant of Jawe." This chosen one is to announce, indeed to bear in hand, a new *florum*, to plant it amid the imperial wilderness, unpromising as is that soil.

The name of the imperial "native growth" is injustice. The name of the imported *florum* is—justice (Isaiah 42:1–4).

✦ ✦ ✦

So our present text would seem to start with a literary fiction. A supposed Solomon addresses, nay urges his peers, to undertake godly ways. The author's intent is modest and realistic. He dwells among a Judaic community dispersed in the imperial orbit. In the way of a Daniel, he must urge vigilance, even wariness: his people must keep an eye open upon their tradition and culture, both.

✦ ✦ ✦

The author of Wisdom however, is hardly in Daniel's precarious position. These Greeks are tolerant, alive in the mind, welcoming of new ideas, a far cry from the dim, vacuous tyranny of Babylon.

First, as to opportunities before them, our author addresses his own community. Its windows are open on the world, the winds blow through. The ambiance of the diaspora is Alexandrian, sophisticated and nuanced of mind. Let the message also include the Greeks, and name them friends.

And as for ourselves, Jews. Let us not hesitate to borrow these grand qualities of our host nation, to our own benefit.

Thus Jews are invited by one of their own, to sip the sublime Greek vintage, to taste its inebriating genius: Homer, Heraclitus, Aristotle, Plato, Sophocles, Xenaphon. The vessel proffered seems bottomless: in it are reflected a lively play of the mind's powers.

✦   ✦   ✦

The terrain is enticing, it promises a transfiguration. Let us Jews, leaning above the lucid waters of Greece, see mirrored there our own image. Let us lean closer, drink deep of this greatness.

But shall we not risk drowning in it? The waters are amnesiac, they bring forgetting. Shall we then forget—God, temple, torah, the liturgy of recalling, the prayer and sacrifice, care of the "widow and orphan and stranger at the gate"?

✦   ✦   ✦

Let us create a fiction of note. Let us place the golden crown of Solomon upon our own brow. Let us assume that the king was an icon of justice, a ruler who merited a respectful hearing, who urged his peers to like works of justice.

Thus the fiction yields its meaning. Revealed is an exhortation, nuanced but unmistakable.

Thus at one stroke, two audiences, Jewish and Greek, are addressed. Let Jews take justice seriously: in their tradition it is a supreme virtue, their offering to the world. And let Greeks as well be reminded of the responsibility, of its sovereign import (and let us go further)—of equal import to Jew and Greek. For matters of justice are pivotal: their skill and practice bespeak the human measure itself.

The Greeks have discussed justice, analyzed it at length. They even claim to have attained it in their political structures, their "demos," the city-state.

✦   ✦   ✦

Perhaps the claim is valid, perhaps not.

We all but note in the text a lifted hand, a hesitation, so Jewish. The thought: Let us go slow. Let us welcome the greatness that surrounds us like a nimbus, let us be grateful for it, study it, emulate it. Let us enter the Greek portals. But let us not be stripped before entering.

Thus, under a stipulation, the author enters the grand portico. Shall we say, by a side door?

Entering, he bids others to follow.

But not for worship. In this regard, we stop short. Greek humanism is one thing, a great and noble. But these people know not God.

✦   ✦   ✦

Can we Jews of the dispersion go further, since by supposition we "know God"? Let this at least be adduced: we are so summoned, so reminded, to "seek God."

The fiction of the author continues. Under the royal vault of Solomon, under his aegis, let it be adduced that all are invited to hearken, to "seek" God.

The Greeks are enchanted by worldly greatness, their own and others'. The name of Solomon sounds in their ears, an audible glory.

The tradition of the Jews is different (but does it have salient likenesses?) The difference: in remembrance lies salvation: the past must be made present. Thus the summoning of Solomon is or may be, a form of anamnesis, a verbal reminder akin to the ritual of Passover or Pentecost.

But a doubt, one hopes a salutary one, persists. Do the likes of Solomon heed the summons to "love justice," to "seek God"?

✦   ✦   ✦

The search written of in the book of Wisdom is also urged by the prophets.

And a question, always a question. On what basis does the author urge that Jews, let alone Greeks, are to "seek God"? A God Who is the utterly Beyond?

A radiant theology of grace is implied. You, Greeks or Jews, would not seek God, had you not already found God.

More exactly, if God had not first found you. There is One Who initiates the "search": Who enables, beckons, disposes, stirs up, grants light, awakens hunger and thirst—Who moves the heart toward further movement.

Reality is in the movement. There is One Who first loves us, that we may love God. One Who "so loved the world," as we Christians know, as to "give His only Son" (John 3:16).

✦   ✦   ✦

1:2 So we begin with this: "God is found by those who do not put the Holy to the test."

It seems instructive and to the point here, that the warning of not "putting God to the test" is addressed to the great ones of the world. And the fiction proposes that the greatest of all, Solomon, here addresses the other great ones of earth: peers, take care!

The irony is striking. There could be no more awesome way of "putting God to the test" than this: to construe a god who resembles one's self, a mirror image of appetite and fanaticism. And worse: to contrive as issuing from this god, a summons to jihad.

✦   ✦   ✦

Alas, in the years of his reign, as is recorded, Solomon frequently put God to the test. In more or less blind imitation of a pharaoh, he honored a deity much to his own inclination. He saw glory in a mirror, and fell—or walked—in.

Madly venturesome or clumsy, sinking in idolatry, he dramatized an ancient fault, as well as a modern—if not a postmodern. Tyrants fantasize then project their god: as real, as true—as their own, their "proper" god: in the sense of private, and a property. An owned god, captive, useful: a genie.

So sinning, the Solomonists find strong support in priestly sycophants, whose interests coincide with those of their royal patron.

Such religion and the *imperium* walk well in tandem. The king even includes the priesthood in the roster of his bureaucracy: service at the altar wraps the priesthood in a golden aureole. And as the song has it, "the living is easy."

So Solomon constructed to the honor of this suitable deity—need it be added, to his own honor and glory?—a celebrated temple. Think big! In pretension and grandeur, his construction rivaled the pyramids.

✦   ✦   ✦

Thus the sojourn of the Jews in Egypt, initiated in shame and enslavement, came to its ironic summing up. After Solomon, the great empire fell in two, a fruit gone to rot.

✦   ✦   ✦

The tale began with shame and confusion. A people were taken captive, enslaved in a foreign land. Eventually they arose, their god impelling, and fled into the desert wilderness, into a promise, a land of their own. Where—on this the record is murky—they disposed of or intermarried with the inhabitants. In any case, this tribe, once indentured, came to a mighty flourishing.

And in time, their behavior began to ape that of their former oppressors. Thus, as the cynic of Proverbs might be led to observe, a circle closed: vanity, all vanity.

✦　✦　✦

This never-ending search and seeking: always the more, the *magis* of the Spiritual Exercises of Saint Ignatius, the stretching of the human to its utmost, implied in the motto of the Order: *ad majorem Dei Gloriam*. We know it. It is a law of the heart, a rhythm of dilation and contraction: the blood races through the body, then subsides and grows steady. From utmost effort to the quotidian. After ecstasy, say the Buddhists, the laundry.

✦　✦　✦

1:3 "Perverse counsels" are darkly native to sons and daughters of the Fall. A base, sleazy argument is decked in robes of office. Now the worst is transformed. It is made to appear the better:

> The president refuses to admit that he lied under oath. It is nearer the truth, he maintains, that he may have somewhat stretched the truth (sic). But there was no least intent to perjure himself (*New York Times*, 12/9/1998: the Impeachment Proceedings).

✦　✦　✦

The Hebrew bible is rife with warning. Only dare to put providential love to the test, and the Omnipotent reacts in fury, confounding the foolhardy. The stories of Exodus told repeatedly of such "testing." Someone (or many) crossed a line, and the violation invariably turned out badly for the presumptuous.

Still, one is baffled: where is that famous line drawn? Is it visible to the eye? And further, how is one to know its location—unless it be by crossing over?

Short of firm prior instruction, there remains a gray area here. Moses, we are told, paid heavily for a mysterious infraction, which the text only hints at. The episode took place at the "waters of Meribah" in the desert. The people were parched. Under instruction, Moses "struck the rock twice with his staff, and water gushed out in abundance . . ."

The matter is left at that. And the question arises: Why the second blow against the rock? Did Moses doubt the power of God?

From the dire outcome we infer that something went terribly awry: the punishment was condign. God spoke:

"You shall not lead this people into the land which I will give them."

Moses and Aaron must die outside, at the portal of the promise. And so it was done (Numbers 20:11, 12).

Is this the intent, that we are to know the default only in its punishment? (and even at that neuralgic point, it often happens that we are given little light!)

✦   ✦   ✦

1:4 We tread deep waters here: it is asserted that wickedness and wisdom are absolutely incompatible. Never can the two, unholy spirit and holy, coexist on one life: any such attempt brings swift catastrophe:

"Nor does wisdom dwell in a body under debt of sin."

A strange expression to be sure, a body "paying tribute" to sin (BJ). Not that the body is declared evil: but "the flesh" can become tyrannical, subjecting the soul to enslavement. Paul knew it: so did the Jesus of John.

We have in Paul's letter to the Romans, a painful, universal, strangely personal analysis of the subjection of the soul to desire. Later, Augustine will enlarge on the subject, the pain, the psychological acumen of Paul.

The apostle for his part sees humans deprived of Christ, like figures turned to fire in a painting by El Greco. The description is a twist of shame, a confession, an unveiling of soul:

> I am weak flesh, sold into the slavery of sin. I cannot even understand my own actions. I do not do what I wish to do, but what I hate. . . .

> I know that no good dwells in me, that is, in my flesh. The desire to do good is there, but not the power. What happens is that I do, not the good I will to do, but the evil I do not intend. . . .
>
> Even though I want to do what is right, a law that leads to wrongdoing is always ready at hand. My inner self agrees with the law of God: but I see in my body's members another law, at war with the law of my mind: this makes me the prisoner of the law of sin in my members.
>
> What a wretched man I am! Who can free me from this body under the power of death?
>
> All praise to God, through Jesus Christ our Lord! (Romans 7:14–25)

First person, third person? Paul speaking of himself, or of others? Of someone inside, outside the orbit of grace?

Taken as an analysis of the human plight, the passage is extraordinary. He speaks of others, he speaks with capacious insight of—himself. He too had known years of being a castaway, this fiery persecutor of the faithful.

No wonder his threnody for the "wretched man that I am," no wonder the praise for a power that struck him flat and raised him up. He underwent a wrenching conversion of heart: nonetheless, the stench of brimstone lingers in his soul.

✦　✦　✦

Jesus holds public debate with religious leaders (John 8:31 ff). Ancestry is in contention. Is it sufficient to invoke a revered patriarch as validating one's status in the world? The religious authorities declare so, with passion: Jesus says them nay, with equal passion.

He goes further, provoking them. In a shocking exposé, a tour de force of insight and courage, He reveals their secret "works." He is a master of irony: these leaders, he declares, "believe" in Him. But the belief is shallow and parched, and masks dark urges.

These must be unmasked, brought to light. The truth demands it:

"If you live according to My teaching, you are truly my disciples: then you will know the truth, and the truth will set you free."

"Set you free?" It stings. Is he implying, "You are unfree," are "slaves"? Their riposte:

"We are descendants of Abraham. Never have we been slaves to anyone."

He will not allow so heavy a claim, so binding, to stand unchallenged.

To the heart of the matter! Their declared discipleship of Abraham is a fraud, a cover for dark designs.

Cast prudence to the winds. Let them know it: He knows what impulses move in them:

"I give you my assurance: everyone who lives in sin is the slave of sin."

Hereditary pride of place is on display. But let it be revealed—the darkness into which pride plunges them:

"I realize you are one of Abraham's stock. Nevertheless, you are trying to kill me, because my word finds no hearing among you."

The truth is out: it is like a blow in the face. These, disciples, these "who believed in him"—and they plot his murder?

Yes. Killing the messenger silences, invalidates once for all, the message. Or so it is designed. The thought is a secret buried in hell, so deeply buried, one surmises, that not one of these disciples of Abraham has revealed it to another.

The revelation is a two-edged blade: it impales and raises before all, a design common to all, but known only to the one harboring it.

Now what to do? It is out, the secret: communality in crime.

There has been much talk of Abraham, many claims, the advantage lent by a noble ancestor and bloodline. Very well then, let Jesus declare his own antecedence:

"I solemnly declare it: before Abraham came to be, I AM."

At that, they picked up rocks to cast at him . . .

Thereby of course, dramatizing the truth of his revelation. Dark desires have shown face.

✦ ✦ ✦

1:5 Worth quoting, worth dwelling upon:

> The holy spirit of discipline
> flees deceit
> and withdraws
> from senseless counsels:
>
> it is set to naught
> when injustice occurs.

How eminently the text befits the Holy Spirit of Jesus, the Spirit who is supreme Teacher of humankind (John 14:26):

> The Paraclete,
> the holy Spirit
>
> whom the Father
> will send in My name

> will instruct you
> in everything
>
> and remind you
> of all I have told you.

And we confess it, lost as we are and only partially found, amid the historical debris of the Fall. We still do not understand. We must await the gift, a rebirth of mind and heart.

Wisdom: no picayune matter, of piety kept close or of virtue untested.

♦ ♦ ♦

The Spirit comes "in My name." Which is to say, revealing the hidden workings of the world—forces concealed from the world itself, even while virulently at work there.

In the era of the Savior's sojourn among us, the supreme "work" of death is the condemnation and execution of Jesus.

And in our day? Weaponry, pouring across the world as though from a tipped bucket of hell. The contempt is palpable, toward the Creator and the works of the Seven Days. The weapons and their makers and purveyors conspire to declare humans and all creation—expendable.

♦ ♦ ♦

Those "works" of the world remain hidden from multitudes of disciples as well, torpid and halfhearted and to this day, "slow to believe."

And then, hope. A people grows "teachable," the Gift is welcomed. And what a profoundly anticultural Gift it is!

One summons to mind the duplicity and moral blindness issuing like a miasma from the highest reaches of American authority. From an imperial apparatus of the Fall, the gift of Wisdom is withheld.

♦ ♦ ♦

The Spirit as Teacher. Once more Jesus speaks:

> When She comes,
> the Spirit of truth,
>
> She will guide you
> in all truth.
>
> She will not speak
> on her own,
>
> but will speak
> only what She hears.
>
> She will announce to you the things to come (John 6:13)

Right thought, right action in the world! How precious that title: "spirit of truth." And alas, as we bitterly acknowledge and even more bitterly experience, in us the Spirit of Truth must wrestle nightlong with the spirit of untruth!

And which spirit is to prevail? We ruefully confess: we can hardly announce with confidence beforehand.

✦ ✦ ✦

Consolation: the Gift is never exhausted, it wells up, poured from a bottomless source, the divine largesse.

The Spirit has "heard": and She speaks. She has heard the word of truth, spoken in the world by Jesus. So she comes to us, single of mind, to make the word reverberate in us, a thunder in the torpid world.

Let this be acknowledged soberly. Whatever might be summed up as the truth of human life, implying access to God, knowledge of the world, self-knowledge—this has another source than the human. And this, no matter what genius, education, advantages of color, or status are adduced.

As for the American ethos, its claim to primacy of place, we have seen enough to distrust it utterly: genius gone awry, gone to rot—in the Pentagon, the Supreme Court, the White House, the "justice system."

✦ ✦ ✦

In the mutual give and take of Bible study and reflection, we have seen divine altruism at work. The Gift is bestowed on those who ponder the text together, time and again, year after year, a rhythm of life itself. A savor, an inner sense, Wisdom streaming from the Creator, to Jesus, through the Spirit, to ourselves.

✦ ✦ ✦

And those "things to come." We wonder, dwelling on this or that scene laid open by the text.

And after the fact, after the transformed lives and labors and deaths of the first disciples of Jesus, we know much that lay concealed from them. We know what "was to come," what fruit of their labors and death.

We know the conclusion of Gospels and Acts and Letters, and beyond.

And hard to acknowledge, is the pattern set in those first years, the evangelical "way" (a neutral term to be sure, only hinting at the explosive reality). A "way" varied in detail of temperament and talent, and varying not at all in essentials of faith—and of consequence.

Today as well, to intuit and embrace the "way" sets the heart alight. To know that it varies not a whit in essentials, from the pattern of those first years.

Faith—and the consequence of faith. In our lifetime. As dramatized in the fate of Christians in Salvador, Guatemala, Nicaragua, Chile, Israel-Palestine, China, East Timor, Sudan.

We know something of the awful drama, its ongoing scene, its consequence.

The freighted "consequence" can hardly be limited to say, Roman gibbets, a coliseum and ravening lions. Other, far different "things to come" as well. Elijah returning, the coming of Jesus, Jerusalem descending from on high, the nations streaming up Mount Zion to acknowledge God.

Violent deaths are endured across the world. And yet, and yet: swords are beaten into plowshares. Far different things to come. And in essence, one and the same.

Images, events. To be summoned, to hearten us. Today, as we dwell, under the volcano of an unknown future. Those "things to come."

The fires of the century have raged. The lava flowed and overwhelmed and left millions of victims, millions of bare survivors: bereft, deprived, a socialized Job.

And what of the fire next time?

✦   ✦   ✦

1:6 Wisdom loves humans: how reassuring!

And how this love resounds in the biblical pages, touching and transforming, reaching into our "reins and heart"!

It is like a light struck in a dark cave. A light cast on the ancient images of the cave wall, which is to say, on the unconscious and conscious activity of soul. A light cast on the mystery of the human.

The Gift of Wisdom is not psychological acuity: it is the discerning skill of a heart open to all weathers, making all weathers from torrid to icy, one.

The Gift enables us to comport ourselves as humans—and this against the odds of an inhuman time.

✦   ✦   ✦

This "friendship with the human" is a constant theme in Wisdom (7:23).

Again, a believer is fully human when behaving justly (12:19). Trusting to this Love, submitting before its suave rhythms, its large benignity, we are not to forget that Wisdom has a firm outline and edge. Not everything befits, not "anything goes": Wisdom also implies judgment. Judgment is laid like a measure against behavior: we are accountable.

✦ ✦ ✦

1:7 A pentecostal utterance:

> The Spirit of the Lord
> fills the universe,
>
> holds
> all things together,
>
> knows
> all forms of utterance.

It would seem that the church is called to this momentous task: to hold close in the Spirit, in honor and unity (and in face of cultural disintegration and incoherence), all that is worthy, all that is encompassed by the noble term *human.*

Thus enabled by the Spirit, let believers respond to the deepest longings of others. In a culture of death, longing for a way out of death, longing for a word of life, for companions who favor and cherish life. For that multitude "clothed in white garments" who surrender life itself for sake of others (Revelation 6:11).

Often we fail, we play the Pharisee, contemn the movements of the spirit in others. This is a required honesty and confession. Let us look to it.

✦ ✦ ✦

1:8 The Spirit who "holds all in unity" is also a Spirit of Justice, personified. This is the Spirit of moral discrimination, the Enlightener of conscience, the One who sets ethical boundaries.

How wonderful to acknowledge the Spirit, engulfed as we are in America in authority which disdains accountability!

We ponder the insight here. The Spirit defines sin, the Spirit acts as Judge. And the Judgment is handed down here and now.

Let it be said simply. Judgment in the Spirit, defining sin, is the responsibility of the believing community. A momentous matter that the prophets clarified, and that Jesus powerfully underscores.

That solomonic priestly definition of sin, as a violation of niceties of liturgical practice—this is abrogated, once for all.

Sin is injustice: sin is the maintaining of systems that create misery, poverty, and war.

War is mortal sin, the maker of "widows and orphans" on a vast scale.

✦ ✦ ✦

Definition, then denunciation: the task of believers. The unmasking of
the interplay of unjust systems. The "woes" of chapter 23 of Matthew's
Gospel bespeak a passionate judgment laid against the structures of
the Fall.

✦ ✦ ✦

1:9 More and yet more concerning judgment. Power is the world's
mighty engine: through it the "dwellers on earth" build and build. Driv-
ing all before, they create a cultural tower of Babel. A demigod
inhabits it.

We witness the event in lamentable days and nights. The imperial tower,
a construct of violence and pride, crumbles before our eyes. The end is in
sight.

✦ ✦ ✦

America has to be founded on a deeply religious faith—
and I don't care what it is.

(Dwight Eisenhower)

✦ ✦ ✦

1:10–11 Ever so subtly the theme "words of the impious" of verse 9 is
clarified. One must beware these "vain murmurs," this "wicked schem-
ing." Surely in the historical books, we have biblical evidence for the
proliferation of both.

And how, according to God's word, are the troublemakers met by
the Deity? With a "jealous ear." God, it would seem, fiercely intervenes.
The shameful murmuring, as occurred at the waters of Meribah
(Numbers 20:11 ff), must be halted.

Likewise, idolatrous or superhuman schemes are brought to naught.
The tower of Babel is raised (Genesis 11): shortly the project falls to chaos.

Communal understanding dissolves like a dream of what never was,
or of what was and is no more.

✦ ✦ ✦

In spite of warnings and disasters, the law of the Fall holds firm, a
death grip on the body of history. Centuries pass, little or nothing of change
of heart.

Towers fall, towering pride stands intact. The "murmuring," a species
of stonewalling in favor of pride of place, continues.

✦ ✦ ✦

Today a notorious, indeed scandalous example comes to mind.

Let numerous American bishops condemn capital punishment, as they do. And let us presume, as is often the case, that the governor of a given state is Catholic. It has become a lethal commonplace: this official ignores the teaching of his Church, and proceeds to sign death warrants. "Murmuring." Moral instruction proves weightless against a raw hundredweight of political ambition.

And the "Tower of Folly" continues to mount heavenward. The builders challenge God with imperial projects: new and ever more deadly weaponry, systems of pretension and domination, idolatry of the dollar. The foundations reach down and down, to hell.

✦ ✦ ✦

Afraid of shadows, retreating further into the realm of increasingly gigantic symbols, we hope to keep ourselves safe from death by embracing, as if they were beloved toys, the images of death. Presuming the presence of nonexistent enemies, we adopt the hypochondriac's device of staging an endless round of preemptive cures, in order to postpone, perhaps indefinitely, our dying of natural causes.

> People do not necessarily like to buy or rent other human beings. To do so, they must repress too much of their own humanity, with the result that they become cold, rigid and scared. But what other choice do they have in a society in which the glorious name of profit justifies squalor, famine, dishonesty and war? The substitution of money for all other systems of value, facilitates the attack on self, on culture, on country, on time past and time future.

(Lewis Lapham, *Money and Class in America*)

✦ ✦ ✦

The imperial system is built on pilings of greed and violence, as Isaiah testifies:

> The land is full
> of silver and of gold,
>
> there is no end
> to their treasures.
>
> The land is full
> of horses,
>
> there is no end to their chariots.

The land
is full of idols,

they worship
the works of their hands . . . (2:7–8)

Exactly.

✦　✦　✦

Sixteen years after President Reagan envisioned a "star wars" program to protect the United States from ballistic missiles attack, President Clinton plans to pledge about $7 billion over six years to build a limited "missile defense system" . . .

And at this point, no one has proved that such a system will work.

Since Mr. Reagan unveiled his dream of creating an impenetrable shield against nuclear missiles in 1983, the nation has spent some $55 billion trying develop a workable weapon—so far to no avail. But never before has any money been put in the budget actually to build one.

(*New York Times*, 1/7/1999)

✦　✦　✦

A moral fabric is being ever so deftly woven. A "stealthy utterance," and a "lying tongue" are impugned. The latter brings "death to the soul."

And how consonant, one thinks, with the teaching of Jesus. He speaks harshly to his detractors:

The father you spring from
is the devil . . .

Lying speech
is his native tongue:

he is a liar
and the father of lies . . .

If I
am telling the truth
why
do you not believe me?

The reason
you do not hear

is this:
you are not of God. . . . (John 8:44–47)

A terrifying indictment, inviting close scrutiny. It is leveled precisely against religious authorities. Their claims of holy ancestry are weightless: they serve only to immunize the heart against the truth.

Let that truth appear in unexpected garb of form or speech: a scandal, an upsurge of revulsion follows. Unpalatable, outrageous—this Jesus, declaring that his existence predates Abraham!

The truth is so new as to be in fact, ancient, primordial. It shakes to pieces every assumption of eminent ancestry and divine favor. What if— but of course the thought is absurd—what if this Jesus were neither mad nor ill founded? And what if we, the chosen, were in the eyes of God, pariahs, enemies of the truth, enemies of grace?

Perish the thought. The tower of pride stands intact.

But what of communality of symbol and speech, the credentials of right reason? These are shaken.

✦ ✦ ✦

We note with awe that the ancient truth has taken human form. This Man who presents himself, likely as not in the conventional garb of a rabbinical gyrovague, who speaks with a Galilean patois, whose family rubs elbows with neighbors like themselves, a people neither wealthy nor politically connected—indeed quite the contrary—this Man is the God who long ago, as Scripture attests, was adored by Abraham?

What are the descendants of Abraham to make of Him? (What are we to make of Him?)

In psychological jargon, his opponents were long conditioned by a belief, implicit but unshakeable: they and their bloodline (a bloodline that became a system) embodied the divine will and word. Blood was their warrant: through it, they were blessed.

Through generations they, their kin and their claim, stood firm. Occasion requiring, they issued an infallible word concerning the deity.

They were, as they firmly believed, authorities of an end time, never to be seriously challenged, let alone superceded. Theirs was the established religion: their piers were deep, sunken in torah and temple, in Abraham and Moses. And what or who was to shake the pillars?

There arrived this Jesus, shaker and breaker—of assumptions, of claims to divine favor by reason of ancestry, temple, torah, priesthood and prophecy, shekinah and pillar of fire, scripture and sabbath and passover—all in sum conferring infallibility, Divine favor beyond cavil. Or so it was said, and written, and preached in season and out.

Into this scene He came, this maestro of a gradual unveiling. First He kept ancestry a secret, like a jewel in a dark corner. With great care, he began prizing open minds and hearts: "What if . . . ? What if . . . ?" First the minds of his own, then the public at large, the "crowd."

Finally He turned to the claimants of torah and temple.

He began questioning: more, casting doubt on such matters as were presumed, for centuries, closed. He brought to a point of eruption, hidden forces of darkness. They surfaced, boiled up and over.

✦   ✦   ✦

Herod and Pilate for their part, were true to form. Which is to say, they acted as indentured slaves of the law of the land, cronies of the temple claque and the occupying power.

Smug mediocrities decreed that the God of heaven must be tried and executed as a common criminal.

Thus far the law: thus far its executors—and its executioners.

✦   ✦   ✦

But the high priest, the Sanhedrin, the entourage of Pharisees and scribes and doctors of the law present a different, more complex and abrasive problem. Grant them their noble due. For centuries their religion had lit and kept alive a light amid surrounding darkness, whether in Egypt or Babylon—or in the Jerusalem of the kings.

Time and again the prophets proclaimed, invariably at cost of favor and repute and of life itself, the truth.

This: the god of the likes of Saul, David, and Solomon was a complaisant captive of imperial designs.

A far different God was entering the world.

Theirs was a perilous undertaking, a mighty purification of the religious sense. Temple religion, as Ezekiel proclaimed, was long gone in idolatry. The god of court and temple, of wars and conquests, served the pretension and pride of the kings.

The prophets were unimpressed, the kings unamused. And a whiplash fell.

✦   ✦   ✦

The likes of Isaiah and Jeremiah and Ezekiel signal two great events: the death of the old god, and the emergence of the God of the prophets.

The prophets proclaimed a birth: more, under God they brought it to pass. The birth of the God of the victimized, of the "stranger at the gate." A God hostile to war, the dark unmaker of humans, fearsome creator of "widows and orphans."

A birth. The God of Jesus, God of the Sermon on the Mount.

✦ ✦ ✦

Two millennia after Jesus, we survey our world.

And what to make of those words of His, counseling nonviolence and love and compassion? They are gingerly shelved, a begrudged, partially ratified manifesto, honored in the breach, contemned in practice.

A "new humanity"? Again and again the promise is stillborn or aborted. Manifesto of the Christian church? We wait so long.

Nevertheless, through the prophets and Jesus, God is reborn. Let us raise a muted alleluia.

✦ ✦ ✦

1:12 We begin a long, subtly nuanced treatment of the principality named death.

"A furtive word" . . . "a lying mouth" . . . "an erring way of life," these are the "second death" of which Revelation speaks.

The tongue embraces the lie. A mask melds with the face. The message becomes the medium, the soul is twisted in a kind of double helix, a form that utters the "furtive word."

What acute understanding, what insight into the soul of dark motive!

✦ ✦ ✦

Destruction comes also, it is noted (though the "also" must be qualified): through "the works of your hands," a reference to idolatry.

A lie becomes a god. It looms and grows: a dead hunk of wood becomes a threatening imperative. It must be worshipped, paid tribute to—the tribute of death.

And inevitably, given the institutionalized, technologized, militarized (the words clank along ponderously, a pretense at invincibility)—given the multiple forms of "the lie" today—the mandated death ("just war, necessary war, inevitable war," etc., etc.) befalls others: the innocent, or those who inhibit or rebuke or stand in the way of the prospering of the lie.

✦ ✦ ✦

Jesus will take up the theme, with passion. Enmity to the truth is a form of death before death:

> Why
> do you not understand
> what I say?

It is because
you cannot bear
to hear My word.

And then, even more fiercely and at length, a diatribe pours out:

The father
you spring from
is the devil,

and willingly
you carry out
his wishes.

He brought death
from the beginning,

and has never
based himself on truth:
the truth
is not in him.

Lying speech
is his native tongue,

he is a liar
and the father of lies.

But because I
deal in the truth,
you give me no credence . . .

If I am telling the truth,
why
do you not believe Me? (John 8:43–46)

✦   ✦   ✦

The questions raised, the passionate assured tone, and especially the implication that the "father of lies" lives and flourishes—in them!

The words were received with fury, as John reports.

Thus the awful indictment. The lie reigned high and mighty, ruled minds and hearts—religious minds to be sure, charged with formation of other minds, these doctors of the lore of the tradition, accustomed to the honor and fealty of all. . . .

Then comes this challenger of temple and state, of state owned temple. He would bring them down.

And his purpose, as they took rueful note, is hardly to include violence (the occupying power having at disposal vastly more weaponry than any band of anarchists could command).

This eruption was far more dangerous. Jesus came with hands extended, palms open, weaponless, accusative, declaring a war of the spirit.

Who owned the tradition? Whose authority held firm?

Theirs, and no other. "We have Abraham for father."

✦   ✦   ✦

Who owned the tradition? Who dared pry open a door since the time of Abraham shut and locked? And more: who dared stand at the open door, a watchman and welcomer, inviting the multitudes within. Declaring: "I AM the door?"

✦   ✦   ✦

He confronted the brute force of the lie, its hold over human life. The lie decreed the death of the mind. It issued a demonic claim.

He was impelled to personify the lie: "the devil." He bestowed on an "it," a bloodline and ancestry. He turned around that vaunted fatherhood of Abraham, as claim and credential: No, theirs was another ancestor, "the father of lies."

Then, having cleared the ground, He launched a lightning bolt. To what compare it, that truth? It was a birth pang in creation. Everything shifted: the closed door opened, the absolute became relative, if not hypothetical.

How dared He? "Before Abraham was, I AM."

The word, the claim (the claim daringly counter to theirs) asserted that the divine came to rest on—Himself. To that degree, it was intolerable. It canceled, or at least rendered questionable, the authority of his adversaries. They were replaced, they were to step down, to start over.

A new Protagonist stood there, a new Lawgiver, another Mediator.

That intolerable *pronunciamento*, preceded by an insulting accusation— your paternity is demonic!

Whom did He make Himself? What were they to make of this new Presence, this Authority arrogating theirs to Himself? The words were blasphemous. They stopped their ears.

Thus the height of the irony encounters the depth of the entrenchment, as the divine enters a Fallen world.

The judgment turned on the Judge: God must be—disposed of.

✦   ✦   ✦

1:13–15 Here personified, ironically one thinks, is Death, an "It" that would be a "He." This pretender to the throne of time and creation—Death —must constantly be pushed back and back.

The words are to be accounted among the most sublime of the Bible, comparable to the utterances of great Isaiah or Job.

✦   ✦   ✦

It is as though the page spontaneously combusted. Before our eyes stands an angel of hope, the revelation: God is the God of life.

In an equally sublime apothegm, Jesus will echo this master of wisdom:

> For God is the God of the living, not of the dead
> (Matthew 22:32)

✦   ✦   ✦

We are urged to pause and ponder: to give the words their majestic due, our reverent, rejoicing attention:

> God
> has not created death,
>
> God does not rejoice
> in the destruction of the living.
>
> No. God has created all
> that all might live.
>
> Creation
> is charged with life,
>
> no poison of death
> infects the living,
>
> Death
> sits no earthly throne.
>
> The just
> are immortal (Wisdom 1:13–15)

✦   ✦   ✦

Clairvoyant, cool, devoid of images. Simply, the master and mystic reports on what he has seen.

What has he seen? He has seen God take death seriously, God analyzing the tactics of death that we too might take death seriously.

Seriously, but not obsessively. For death is here declared penultimate, even redundant. Therefore a contrary urging: that we take life with far greater seriousness than death.

To stand where God stands: for life.

✦ ✦ ✦

Meantime, in the awful crepuscular "meantime" that defines our era,
death is no mirage, no folkloric monster. Death wears faultless military
garb, or elegant civilian garb. So guised (and disguised), and with inde-
scribable military and economic violence at its behest, death cuts a swath
both wide and terrible.

A claim is trumpeted across time and "the four-cornered world." A
given war (any war), is "just," "necessary," "virtuous." Or again (and the
same assaulting claim)—"world markets? they exist and flourish to the
benefit of all."

Thus the lie that justifies the murder, the international larceny, the
sweatshops and child labor, the indenturing of the poor. Thus too, the
gods of death, their works and pomps concealed (to most, save the vigilant and the victims).

They would persuade us: yield to enslavement of spirit.

The claim of death is brutal and plausible. Across the world images of
triumphant death are raised on high. Weapons, monuments, bemedaled
generals, complaisant authorities push the ideology hard.

Eschewing accountability and judgment, the masters of the security
superstate wreak human and ecological disaster. Weaponry, more and more
of it: creation insulted, plowshares turned to swords, an "arms race"
unending—a race to oblivion.

Death is both message and media, an absolute empery (or so it is
declared in a thousand tongues and gestures, images and enticements,
threats and bribes)—an absolute empery over life.

✦ ✦ ✦

The biblical "instruction" goes further. The Fall has defined creation
anew—as an ecology of death. The living are in bondage to the gods of
death: on command and therefore, die!

But the wise, so to speak, know otherwise. They take their stand on the
word of God:

> God
> has not created death.
>
> God
> does not rejoice
>
> in the destruction
> of the living.

We have it plain and direct, the implication. The task of the wise is this: to reclaim the world.

Better, to know that the God of life has already reclaimed the world:

> God
> has created all
>
> that all
> might live.

Step into this vast circle of life, embrace life, bestow life!
Reclaim, reconstitute the world.

The irrefutable good news: the throne of death, firm amid a ruined paradise, is toppled. Know it then, behave as though you had witnessed the dethroning of the tyrant:

> Death
> sits no earthly throne.
>
> The just
> are immortal.

We linger over that last sentence, we savor its ambrosial promise.

For our days, it is like a banner held high amid the wreckage of a technological "paradise" gone to ruin.

And if it be true that "the just are immortal"—what of the unjust? Theirs, it is implied, is the 'second death," the death of their humanity. They die even as they kill, they die before death.

But for the just, the outcome is other. "The just are immortal." And what stronger warrant, one thinks, and more comforting, for those who "keep at it," who "walk the talk"!

Christian scripture echoes the style and elaborates the substance of our words of Wisdom:

> This
> we proclaim to you . . .
>
> What we have heard,
>
> what we have seen
> with our eyes,
>
> what we have looked upon
> and our hands have touched—
>
> we speak
> of the Word of life (1 John 1:1–2)

✦ ✦ ✦

The passages, Hebrew and Christian, are remarkably similar. Each falls upon the ear, a simple, majestic, unadorned statement. No nuances, no tropes or images: telegraphic, an epiphany, a handsel.

✦ ✦ ✦

One summons an analogy, the vision accorded Moses. He is admitted to the divine Immediacy, to ecstasy on the mountain. Then he descends and recounts to the waiting people the ineffable Event. In our verse too, words all but fail (but they must not fail). Even as likenesses fall away (they must fall away).

Ex umbris et imaginibus in veritatem—"from shadows and images, to the truth."

Say it, again and again, the mantra. The fate of the gods of death is sealed, they are redundant, finished with.

We, the believing community, witness the Presence of another God than the regent of death. "What we have seen and heard. . . ."

Swords shall yield to plowshares.

The promise, and: "Peter, put up your sword."

And more: "This is my body, broken for you." Behold the God who gives life, rather than taking life. The God of life standing by His word, His deed.

✦ ✦ ✦

1:16 The images that follow deserve the honored term archetypal, foundational. They tell of a world resolutely opposed to the community of faith. That community, it is implied, must be skilled in the arms of the spirit. And knowledge of sin is an element of its wisdom.

The sin? It is wreaked against the just. This is the badge, a stigma.

It shows two faces: holiness and the sin that presses close.

In a kind of last-ditch encounter, the wicked, armed with abusive power, hail the just one to judgment. Archetypal, we suggested, this "justice" of the world, in full panoply.

The revelation is of an anti-revelation, an irony of note. Truth told, the world is capable—and here at last, the truth is told—is capable of a supreme injustice, masked by a supreme fiction.

The injustice is this: the world persecutes and kills the witnesses. The fiction: the just are dealt with in "courts of law," "upholding the law of the land."

Therefore, as the world adduces, it acts justly, its systems weigh right and wrong, and requite with equity.

✦ ✦ ✦

Instructive. The church has seized on the words of Wisdom for its own. To convey this truth: worldly systems, including systems of justice (per- ?
haps the most wickedly skilled of all), are inherently unjust, antihuman. •
Which is to say, they are given over to the purveying and simultaneous masking, of death.

Justice, it proclaims. Injustice it jealously guards, produces.

Let us then, says the Church, tighten the coil. Let us confess the truth, and more: let us dramatize it.

The Fallen world illustrates in its systems the lore and love of death. To this hellish point, this blasphemy. Should God—"per impossible," for the world cannot believe in such an Event—should God enter time and this world and ignite a very blaze of justice and compassion, a gavel will fall. The holy One will be destroyed.

✦ ✦ ✦

Thus the borrowed image, our midrash. The fate of the just One, told here as a conspiracy of the powerful, serves our anamnesis of the passion and death of Christ. The image, we suggested, is primordial. It serves and serves, it is never done with, never proven redundant. Does Christ fall to the "sword of the systems"? He does.

And not only He. In a fallen world, many must fall: Christ is the "first of many brothers and sisters." The pursuit and destruction of the just con-tinues: it is the grist of the mills of history, empire after empire, army after army, "justice systems," death rows, abortion abattoirs . . .

✦ ✦ ✦

The word of God, a two-edged sword, moves in two directions.

In the preceding verses, God has stood revealed as the God of life, in combat with the gods of death. And further: the word of God reveals the vocation of the just: to stand witness for life, thereby attaining godliness.

Now an additional insight. God reads the inmost thought of the ungodly, their version of the "good life."

✦ ✦ ✦

We dwell in a world where Death mightily presumes dominion. Its powers announce it, enact it.

In such a world it is mortally dangerous to play the gull, the beguiled. No, it is incumbent on the just to be wily as serpents, to know of sin and wickedness—even as God knows these.

Sin, wickedness: God goes so far, is so daring!

We have here a kind of "breaking and entering," an ironic "posses-sion" of the wicked and this not by demonic forces. By divine. In this wise: let me, God, read such hearts, enter their dark declivities. And let evil show its face: this for sake of the just, for sons and daughters redeemed. That these be enlightened, and know these *magisters* of death for what they are.

Look closely, be not deceived. These "wicked ones" are in concert: their power is institutionalized, normalized, justified. They wear a public face, carefully assumed: a look of rueful innocence. Believe us, trust us. Can anyone be thought to doubt our benign intent, our zeal for the commonweal?

They speak fervently of vast projects beneficial to humankind. Mean-time, lightning bolts fall. Like forces of nature, catastrophes follow their decisions—bombings, the death of children and the aged and infirm. These are accepted as "givens," as though the punishment of the innocent dif-fered not a whit from a cyclone or tidal wave.

The latest incursion inspires on the part of most, no scrutiny of motive or behavior. The great ones are in charge. The passive and mute go about other concerns.

✦   ✦   ✦

And those notorious courts of law. This is their decor: robe, gavel, mar-shals, handcuffs, "All rise, hear ye hear ye." These wield a vast authority, declare guilt and innocence, dispose of just and unjust.

Are you innocent or guilty? The law of the land will declare it or deny it.

And lo! a transformation: the guilty stand like a primordial Adam, newly wrought.

The innocent before God? Those whose consciences lead them to con-front the law? (Let us say, the law which protects weaponry of indiscriminate destruction? Let these beware: the law of the land has negated that claim: they stand condemned.)

A verdict nears. To mark the moment, it is as though a subaltern were to cast handfuls of dust in the air. The sentencing may then proceed in a cloud of incoherence and vengeance.

✦   ✦   ✦

On our page of the Bible, we catch the wicked in conspiracy, as a plot incubates. Their cover is broken. They are prey to despair, furious and malevolent. Vast power and yet, despair: a lethal mix.

According to this astonishing diagnosis, the powerful-wicked are a hyphenated phenomenon.

A nice implication to be sure, as to the nature of sin: such as these have simply given up on life and the living, on creation and Creator.

Horrific behavior follows: they would deprive others of life.

And not just "any others." The prized victims are the just.

✦ ✦ ✦

How near and dear, how cozened and cajoled, is Death! The images are repellant and enticing, both.

First let us summon the noblest urges of the heart, let one human seek another in affectionate bonding. Then let us turn the images around: before us is a world of depravity and death.

Summon that irony! *Eccolo*, Death the beloved, the friend. Death sets the heart to pining. Death is a streetwalker passing, then beckoned within ("with gesture and voice"). Go further. Tighten the irony to the breaking point. The faithful are joined to God by covenant: that is our dignity, it is also a source of moral understanding. Which is to say, we acknowledge in analogy a marriage bond, God in love with ourselves. The wedding is celebrated by the prophets in ecstatic verse. It is the very "song of songs" of humanity. And we are summoned to lead our lives accordingly, faithful to the bond.

Very well then. Let us borrow that image: bond, vow, pact, covenant. The image is foundational: it illumines our place in the world, our community, our being—we, the beloved of God.

✦ ✦ ✦

Now, let us indict the world in its most grandiloquent form, the empire. The charge? They dare ape God. They have made a pact, vow, bond, covenant—with Death. Theirs is the blasphemy, a larceny committed against hope.

Plunge the knife of truth deep. Then twist the blade:

. . . because they deserve to be Death's possession.

Possession: the word is deliciously ambiguous. The empires and their systems are the rightful property of Death: death is "proper" to them, a native element and setting.

Or: death fits, like a fine glove a hand. Or this: death—befits.

The systems and their devotees are possessed by, invaded by, broken and entered by—Death. As by a demon. We have here the politics of empire laid bare. The imperial systems—economic, military, diplomatic, religious—these serve the efficient, even virtuous functioning of death. They inflict death, they justify it with falsity, pretense, cover, and metaphor. Death never looked so good, so necessary, so regretfully inevitable, as when it rises to the lips of its acolytes, an invocation and incantation. Then the images and words win the day, the polls and applause. "Of course, of course—now we see!"

✦   ✦   ✦

But the above is not the whole story. There is also the following, the unmasking and undoing of Death:

In the early morning hours of December 19, 1999, four members of the "Plowshares v. Depleted Uranium," disarmed two A-10 Thunderbolt planes, nicknamed "Warthogs," at Warfield Air National Guard Base in Essex, Maryland.

The statement of the four (Elizabeth Walz, Philip Berrigan, Stephen Kelly, S.J., Susan Crane):

> —Attack a village with an A-10 Warthog and leave a trench.

> —Attack a village with an A-10 Warthog firing depleted uranium, and leave a poisoned graveyard—the people dead, plants dying or sterile, the earth eternally toxic.

> —The A-10 is an aircraft built around a gun . . . (that) can spew 3,900 rounds per minute. This criminal plane fired 95 percent of the depleted uranium deployed by the U.S. during the Gulf War, leaving behind 300–800 tons, poisoning humans and the elements in Kuwait and Iraq. . . .

> —Depleted uranium is a "delayed response weapon" which burns its way through tank armor and oxidizes, throwing radioactive particles as far as 25 miles . . . . causing somatic and genetic trauma. Cancer often results.

> —The wars in Iraq and Yugoslavia are templates, blueprints for future wars, targeting a total society, military, civilians, the unborn, the infrastructure, the ecology, the health and spirit of a people . . .

> —Ironically, these wars are waged against the troops who fight them. 90,000 Americans are now chronically ill . . . The children of 67 percent of these afflicted veterans were born with severe illnesses or birth defects. . . .

> —This year, Advent, a time of reparation and conversion, ends on December 19. We mark this day by mourning the civilians killed in American wars: nine civilians to every soldier. We also symbolically convert these hellish instruments of death. The "enemy" civilians die forgotten and alone: no grateful nation sorrows at their passing, no flags or official rituals. They are expendable, the true cannon fodder. . . .

✦　✦　✦

Chapter two is low in spirit. And one thinks: how could it be otherwise, as the author sets out to analyze a perverse, malignant despair.

We suggest three stages of this acute psychological probe.

Verses 1–5: "Brief and troubled is our life": which is to say, human life as such. The speakers are the preeminent "dwellers on earth," given over to time and this world. This lifetime, this culture, these possessions are all our portion.

Can it be that there exists another world, a world of spirit, mystery, soul? Can it be that God exists? The questions are beneath serious attention.

We recall that the speaker(s) are the power brokers, the makers and shakers of the world. They presume, as is their wont, to speak for all.

For believers as well? Perhaps the author urges a gesture of recoiling.

Verses 6–9: "Come then, let us make the most of the moment . . ."

Why dwell on time past? And who can know the future? And what of others, of the neighbor? The questions never arise.

Meantime, it is as though the author sounds a tocsin, and a hymn is struck up, adroit, mocking, playful. Let us too, as though joining in the theme of these eminences, celebrate a culture of appetite, consumption, violence!

"With the ardor of youth . . ." The nuances are delicious: time is on the wing, youth is all.

The mick-mockery is delightful. Sing it out: pluck ye rosebuds while ye may!

Verses 10–20: We come to the heart of the matter: the stilled heart. The works are those of death.

We also note the subtle gloss on chapter 1 verses 13–16.

"God has not created Death." Awfully, as our Bible constantly asserts, the works of death flourish in the world—and this in despite of, in contempt of the divine plan. As to abortion, war, capital punishment—no Divine complicity can be adduced. Let the masters of life know it: responsibility rests on them and their monstrous decisions.

Thus we are offered a cultural analysis, acute and skilled. We note the sequence: a frivolous despair, followed by works of death.

✦　✦　✦

2:10 Onto those works.

But first, who are these fervent speechifiers? We are told of a number of renegades, going counter to the community of faith. Their voices suggest a kind of supreme court of the land. They speak confidently and in concert: no dissidents on the high bench.

Condemnation follows: it is plenary, summary, ill tempered, falling on the prey of this "justice system."

We note the one declared guilty: "the just one who is needy," at first glance a curious phrase.

These judges are in contemptuous denial of the divine promise, repeatedly offered in Scripture:

> Neither
> in my youth
>
> nor now
> that I am aged,
>
> have I seen
> the just forsaken,
>
> nor his descendants
> begging bread (Psalm 37:25)

The "choral sin," on the other hand, is celebrated, even gloried in. A system of injustice and greed strips the just of needful goods and services. Workfare, no welfare, the scrapings and gleanings, a grudged charity, no justice!

And we pause: is the author merely reporting, or is he taking sides?

Let the powerful beware exulting: danger lurks. They walk so confidently!

And it may be that in our text, under guise of "objectivity," a volatile critic of works and pomps is announcing their delicts abroad. Let the potential threat not be underestimated. These "widows and the white-haired aged," despised as riffraff and malcontent—it may be that these have gained a hearing.

✦ ✦ ✦

2:11 These mandarins seize on revered prophetic realities, and twist and deface them. They grow unrecognizable:

Let our strength be the (sole) law of justice . . .

The pursuit here, as goes without saying, is something entirely other than justice. The "strength" of the powerful is "the law of the land," that canopy woven of violence and greed, the enemy of biblical justice.

✦ ✦ ✦

For all the attempt at a pious cover, the hypocrites give themselves away. Laconic, cynical the reasoning:

" . . . for weakness proves itself useless."

Possession, nine points of the law. And are the great ones not in possession, wielding the gavel or the sword or the swag—or all three? Wickedness pays off, handsomely. Behold and admire! Those to whom moral or immoral behavior are negotiable items—they rise and shine.

And as for the "just needy one," too bad. He has little to offer the shady "system." Let him be despised, as powerless and an outsider—with a worse fate to follow.

✦   ✦   ✦

The resource of these chameleon consciences, shall it be named? The nub of the matter: the law, the law! The wicked, for once, are right. The law vastly supercedes conscience.

And a further irony, as matters unfold.

Tables are turned: despite the power and might of the law, the derided "weakness" of the just proves an inviolable strength. It shows forth in integrity, honor, forthright speech.

✦   ✦   ✦

2:12 Now comes the charge, purportedly legal (certainly lengthy!), the bitter fruit, it would seem of a smoldering resentment. And to be noted: the guilt and conviction of the just are a foregone conclusion (2:10):

Let us oppress the needy just one.

Venom charges the air. Prior to any stated charges, the wicked collude in the outcome (2:11):

Let us beset the just one . . .

✦   ✦   ✦

One hesitates to draw hard and fast analogies. Still, one detail is remarkable. The chorus that overwhelms the "just needy one"—the accusers, judges, prosecutors, executioners—these are not Pilates, clones of Caesar, pagans. They are believers turned renegade. The awful point hardly seems a matter of chance, or a rare deviance.

✦   ✦   ✦

The past isn't dead. It's not even past.

(*William Faulkner*)

Believers turning renegade? Today, the event invites a question of some moment: are quondam believers (or even declaredly active believers), having won political office, capable of outrageously immoral behavior?

They are. Numbers of "Catholic" leaders uphold pro abortion laws:

others endorse capital punishment. Small matter to these officials that their bishops announce the moral teaching of the Church. Small matter, or none at all.

And what of those Catholic judges and prosecutors, invariably appointed to convict and jail sisters and brothers in the faith, including the nonviolent Plowshares resisters? Remarkable, their fervor. They "do their job" with gusto and aplomb. To their mind, a sense of prestige and responsibility goes far beyond the limits of their office. They are champions of the faith: they hold the keys of the realm of God.

Let them display for all to see, an unexampled severity toward these pretenders, the defendants before us. Nullifying their claim to conscience or bible or international law or this or that justification. In sum, stripping them and their actions of plausibility.

The judges are religious autarchs. They would show the ambit of the True Church—and the false.

✦   ✦   ✦

This "just needy one" refuses to vanish. He stands at the back of the mind, in the shadow of the "justice system," a haunting reproach.

And the irritation is the more galling, one thinks, as memories mock. Did not the accuser once stand in synagogue side by side with the accused? Were they not neighbors, and more—brothers in common symbol and law and worship? Did they not together recall saving interventions from on high?

Those portentous memories, the suave, bracing communalities of Tents and Pasch and Yom Kippur and Hanukah, of holy Law and prophet—all doubling the heart's might!

Gone, and worse than gone: turned to gall and wormwood.

Beyond belief (in more senses than one!)—the contempt shown the "just needy one" matches the reproach of Egyptian tyrants, of Babylonian, and later, Roman.

Matches? No, it surpasses. With venomous will, it would wreak vengeance.

✦   ✦   ✦

But vengeance for what crime, what affront? In such a world, in such inflamed minds, the "crime" adduced expands into a very litany of offenses. The just one "opposes our actions," he "reproaches us for sin." And more, and worse: he "professes to have knowledge of God" and "calls himself servant of the Lord."

Christians will come on the passage, the conspiracy against the just one, with a shock of recognition: it offers a midrash of the fate of Christ.

✦ ✦ ✦

The charges hold no water.

The accused in effect impedes the prospering of the high and mighty. He reserves the right to criticize, even to discredit—and this in light of the Law. He hesitates not at all to accuse the accusers: they have betrayed the tradition and discipline.

✦ ✦ ✦

2:13 But the most galling accusation of all is this: the just one "professes" that he, not the high and mighty, " . . . . has knowledge of God."

A curious point, since, from what can be gleaned from the text, these Jewish accusers have renounced monotheism.

(In favor of what Hellenist school or creed, we are not told.)

Possibly it is not in the purview of the author to clarify where the renegades have landed. Only traces and hints lie on the text, of this or that influence, eudaimonism, stoicism, the tragedians, Xenophon.

(Enough to know the bitter truth: certain Jews have abandoned the faith, and turned with a vengeance against the faithful.)

✦ ✦ ✦

The dossier of charges continues. The defendant styles himself "son of God." "Son," and not "servant": an intolerable self-aggrandizement and a reproach, all wrapped in one.

The wicked fancied themselves an irreducible center: to them and no others, those of right mind tend. From themselves sense and logic proceed.

And woe, the presumptuous one ignores them, draws a circle about himself, makes of himself a new center, a circumference and boundary. He would own the tradition.

And the accusers? They are stigmatized, outsiders, renegades.

✦ ✦ ✦

This turning of the tables, dethroning the enthroned: one finds it delicious and dangerous, both.

Today too we see a similar spectacle, loaded with irony. Courts, judges, prosecutors. And against the accused, the law is mustered in full array.

The charges? Ridiculous in context, severe in potential outcome. Our friends of the "Plowshares" movement have "entered a conspiracy" to "damage government property."

Of course they did, pouring vials of their blood over weapons of mass destruction, wielding household hammers against a destructive technology.

And the law comes down, a furious indemnity. These criminals must pay up, and dearly.

We take note of a further offense: their demeanor. In court they stand uncowed.

Indeed if permitted (it is never permitted) they would turn tables and accuse their accusers. They would present themselves as upholders, defenders, guardians—of international law, of the "provision of necessity," of the moral teaching of the Bible, of conscience itself. They would indict American systems of secrecy, surveillance, duplicity, unexampled violence. Would indict a government whose legal contrivances seek to criminalize them.

In their view, the government is a technological terrorist. Its weaponry threatens its own citizens, children, the ecology, the survival of creation.

✦ ✦ ✦

What is the purpose of technological society?

The only answer modern history has offered . . . is the one Alfred Kazin proposes in *The Great War and Modern Memory:* "War may be the ultimate purpose of technological society."

Experience has a way of sharpening grammar.

Put it plain: "War is the ultimate purpose of technological society."

✦ ✦ ✦

2:14–20 Further and further, the offenses of this "needy just one."

These are as it were, asides: they cannot be thought of as included in a formal indictment. In the offended great ones, ridicule, outrage, anger boil away.

The charges imply an irony, to this effect: a powerless worthless fellow (we remember their dictum: "what is weak is useless")—this one actually thinks himself superior to us!

✦ ✦ ✦

The author, an omniscient observer, knows that the outcome is inevitable. More (and surely a mark of psychological genius), he intuits the process leading to the dénouement.

The gears of the system grind on. The indictment is a cover for the darkest of motives: hatred. Thrones are shaken, the judges and prosecutors stand in the eye of the accused as lesser beings: they are weighed there, and found wanting. Intolerable!

This too is implied. Despite a show of power and might, the day of the great ones is past. Memories are embittered by contrary events, pride of place is toppled. It is they who stand under judgment.

✦ ✦ ✦

During the trial of the "Depleted Uranium Four," in Baltimore, March 2000, Douglas Rokke was summoned by the defense as an expert witness. Rokke is former project director on Depleted Uranium, United States Army, in uniform since 1967, and a professor of environmental science at Jacksonville State University. In the course of the trial, he was not allowed to state the following, which he later wrote:

> The recent trial in Baltimore County . . . demonstrated again that U.S. officials will avoid acknowledging any adverse health or environmental effects, for political and economic reasons. . . . The U.S. deliberately used d.u. in Iraq, Kuwait, Okinawa, Kosovo, Serbia, Bosnia, Puerto Rico and within the U.S. Thousands have been exposed and today many are sick or dead.

> D.U. is a health hazard if it is inhaled, ingested, or gets in wounds. . . . Irrefutable evidence suggests that adverse health and environmental effects occur, unless all contamination is removed.

This evidence was willfully suppressed during the trial . . .

✦   ✦   ✦

To complete the record.

As of June, 2,000, Douglas Rokke has paid dearly for his efforts to get the truth heard. On his return to Jacksonville, he discovered that his home had been invaded and his files seized. Then he was fired from his teaching position. In the ensuing days, he and his family received a number of threatening phone calls, anonymous.

✦   ✦   ✦

To our text. What of the victim, we ask, what of the humiliated, nameless character standing in the dock?

An apotheosis! Sacred books are named for Him, multitudes of saints and heroes follow in his steps. It is he who renews the earth, whose memory and example withstand the assault of the ages. His story creates a myth, a ritual, he breathes soul into the future. No wonder we Christians hold the text in honor. It concerns our Christ:

"My body given for you, my blood poured out for you."

In the world, murder is legitimated.

But the manna falls and falls. And the cup never runs dry.

✦   ✦   ✦

Another image. One must dig deep, search out the "bottom," that awesome source. And stand there, and drink. Thence flows and brims the waters of Jacob's and Jeremiah's well, the promise of the "living water which I shall give."

No wonder the confidence of our Plowshares prisoners. They have tasted the source.

✦   ✦   ✦

And what of those non charges, those thoughts revealed? We ponder: how pique can turn murderous!

> He
> is a living reproach
> to our thinking,
>
> his very presence
> is burdensome,
>
> His way of life
> jarring,
>
> his conduct
> eccentric (2:14–15)

And then an admission that shames and inflames, both. The great ones, the unaccountable judges, are held in a kind of muted contempt. They know it, it is all but beyond bearing:

> To him
> we are
> a debased coinage,
> he avoids us
> like a plague (2:16)

We stand in a world of testing. It is a debased world, delineated with an ironic twist. Authority has turned rotten, scapegoating flourishes. For awhile.

We, together with the defendant, must be patient, awaiting the break-through. We know what the antagonists do not know: or what they suspect and desperately try to forestall. We know of a reversal of fortune.

It is the victim who will emerge as victor. Powerless, invincibly just, this one is the human "type," the icon of the future. This one we observe closely and learn from—and trudge after.

The persecutors? They hold no interest. They are clones of fate, slaves of the realm of necessity. They "front" for the Fall.

The point of their existence is the task they bend to, both demeaning and demonic: the testing of the just one—his fidelity and steadfastness.

✦ ✦ ✦

Look how the accused shows a further grim offensiveness:

> She proclaims
> the final prospering
> of the just,
>
> She boasts
> that God is her father (2:16)

The autarchs in effect have yielded the day: this "just one," measured by her own claim, cannot be defeated.

And what if that claim be true? And more: what if she embodies the claim? What if it be she, not they, who shows forth human greatness, invincible though put to shame?

And that claim of being a divine daughter, how it stings! When all else fails, when the accused stands devoid of succor, her cause doomed—she makes an about-face, she turns to God.

The conclusion of the affair is intolerable—and inevitable. This: the masters of the universe are fated to sit in the school of their would-be victim, to take from her knowledge of God, of conscience, of the human condition.

✦   ✦   ✦

Unwitting or witting, the accusers give themselves away. "Let us . . ."
The treacherous proceedings are stripped to the bone. We hear no formal
charges, no countering of the defense. No trial. How could there be a trial,
since there was no crime?

Let it be said plain. This is legalized lynching.

✦   ✦   ✦

With some relief, we note here an echo of the "trial scene" of the Suffering Servant of Isaiah, chapter 53.

There, to all intents, chaos and incoherence are the implied hallmarks
of imperial "justice." Charges are muddy, a rant of theologizing is loosed,
a cover for malice and the spirit of vengeance. No foundation is laid, no
excuse offered for punishing the guiltless one.

✦   ✦   ✦

Here, what contrast! We are in a fierce high noon of crisis and resolu-
tion: no shadows. The author artfully pierces a decor of pretense, of "justice."
Say it plain, he insists: torture, death, is the project at hand.

Rather than a courtroom, a more accurate scene would be an Elizabe-
than scaffold or an Inquisitional auto-da-fé.

Baldly stated, the intent:

> Let us then see
> if her claims are true,
>
> let us see
> the end of this affair.
>
> If the "just one"
> is a daughter of God,
>
> God
> will succor her,
>
> will deliver her
> from the hands of foes.

The terror of this testing! Terror, but not impelled by the fate of the
just—we know that outcome, its grandeur, its exemplary force and prevailing.

No wonder numerous early Christian writers have seized on verses
12–20 as a noble exposition of the final days of Christ, the "needy just
one." The lines befit the dark motivation that fuels His detractors and
prosecutors.

The Savior goes to his death. And the evangelists (this would seem a sensitive detail of style), make no attempt to penetrate the mind and heart of the Savior. Austerely, the Condemned is left to Himself.

And we? We stand at a distance from this sanctum, the holy of holies where Jesus communes with God and wrestles the demons of the Fall.

Let the gospels record the narrative step by step, his silence, his sparse words.

✦   ✦   ✦

Still, we would know more of this dark collusion of the principalities of state and temple, the forces that conspired in removing the holy One from this world.

In this episode of Wisdom, by way of allusion and analogy, we come on a hint, a clue. The destruction of the just one is wrought by a conspiracy, truculent, hallucinatory, treacherous:

> Let us see
> whether
> his words be true . . .
>
> Let us
> put him to the test . . . (2:17)

Finally the pact is sealed. The dominant powers, whatever their private wars, are agreed on this: the just One must die.

> Let us
> condemn him
> to a shameful death (2:20)

✦   ✦   ✦

It is as though the word of Paul concerning human guilt is being verified, finally, terribly, in the "case of Jesus Christ." Verified, and more: in the court of Pilate and Herod and the outcry of the priests—guilt is horridly dramatized.

In rabbinic fashion, Paul quotes the Hebrew bible as clinching his midrash (Psalm 14):

> There is no just man,
> not one—
> there is no one
> who understands,
>
> no one
> in search of God.
> All have taken
> the wrong course,

> all alike
> have become worthless,
>
> not one acts uprightly,
> not one . . .

Then Paul speaks flatly on his own. It is like a final obit of the human venture:

> All have sinned,
> all are deprived
> of the glory of God (3:23)

But quick! This rabbi is a master of irony and reversal of fortune, of contradictions and mutualities, the interplay of hopelessness and hope.

Abruptly, it is as though as stone were rolled back. A single verse cancels the obituary. Death on rampage, is denied his prey.

> Death is put to death:
> All,
> apart from deserving,
>
> are justified
> by the gift of God . . . (3:24)

✦ ✦ ✦

Our present text is inexorable: we hear much of the machinations of the wicked. An ancient scriptural implication is in the air: the wicked are ignorant of the evil they wreak, the dark night of motive. Only the just have access to that mind and mindlessness. For our instruction.

"Only the just:" which is to say *in casu*, our author, standing as he does at the side of the assaulted "poor just one." Just, anonymous (perhaps deliberately so), an impassioned moralist in the tradition of the prophets, our author is a defender and amanuensis of the nameless "poor one."

We think of him as a kind of Baruch. He deserves a kind of Jeremiah.

✦ ✦ ✦

2:21–24 Therefore, let us hear directly from our author, as he issues a moral codicil on the conspiracy, a judgment against the judges. A relief as well from the brutal scramble of this "testing" by renegades and their pagan allies.

Careful and precise, watchful and wise, quill in hand, sits God's earthly amanuensis, speaking in His name.

To this astonishing scribe, our fervent gratitude. For this: in effect, he confesses to the presence of God in the fallen word: there exists "One who judges."

Lucid, to the point, his moral comment. Lapidary and recondite, he illumines this or that aspect of oppressive evil—behavior that derides God's justice: and all unwitting, mocks the agents of evil themselves.

Wickedness blinds the moral sense. These persecutors lack respect for "the hidden counsels of God" (which, in all their modesty, the author will presently celebrate). They know nothing of the holiness they assault, nor of its divine recompense. Nor, quite another matter, and ominous, nothing of the accounting that lurks!

✦   ✦   ✦

A magnificent resume of the wisdom of Genesis, a vindication as well of that teaching. To wit: in violating the just one, the wicked have violated biblical truth.

This truth. Humans partake of the incorruptibility of God, created as we are in that supernal Image.

The devil, alas, entered the garden where immortals dwelt. These godly ones were hateful to his eyes: let them be brought down.

And what of the contemporary wicked ones? They align themselves with the ancient project: destroy, blight the Image. Bring humans down and down, to death.

✦   ✦   ✦

Thus an ancient wisdom is underscored and brought to bear.

This is the human story, never done with, never finally resolved—the biography of the tribe, woeful and glorious, both. The saints are tested in the fires of tribulation: they taste the original malice, a poison brewed against life and its Author.

And the fires under the brew are hardly to be thought lit by mischance: the wicked stoke them, in the name of a god of their own devising.

✦   ✦   ✦

The conclusion is both mysterious and magisterial:

"They who are in the devil's possession, experience death."

One pauses in wonderment and gratitude. How true the statement, on how many levels of truth!

The equating, first of all, of death and demons—and to this audacious point: the Devil is personified, is perceived as a rational being, obsessed by the blight that lies on him, the death he deals.

We are not to ignore the social implications of "Death" and "Demon," their seizure of the garden of creation and the erstwhile immortal humans. Thereafter "all, all is changed." Women, men, children, the unborn, powerful or victims, lie under the decree of the Realm of Necessity.

The executioners taste death like an ash in the mouth, even as they court death, multiplying its metaphors and means.

To this end (to this day): that death be socialized and normalized, rendered meet and righteous as an instrument of governance. Death: "the way things are."

✦   ✦   ✦

In time, the "dwellers" create a master image of creation itself: a vast laboratory of Mars.

According to this version, "Wickedness" festers in the world, always elsewhere, through a shadowy unnamed "them." Therefore the logic, the imperative, the necessity (that word again) of weaponry multiplied, refined, deployed, huckstered.

The laboratories have their "outlets," the world arms trade, weapons bought, traded, sold across the counters of the world. A burgeoning death culture of weaponry and war, the credential, the badge of belonging to the "club."

✦   ✦   ✦

Innocent as the three famous monkeys, guns see no evil, speak no evil, hear no evil.

Guns believe in guns, guns hope in guns, guns adore guns. In the new dispensation, these are honored as "theological virtues."

There are loving marital guns. They vow fidelity, each to the other, at the altar of revolution. Thereupon they are blessed by clerical guns in white surplices.

Also guns are laid on the table at Mass, next to the bread and wine: then they are said to be transubstantiated, consecrated guns.

There are guns held by sheep and guns held by goats. To the former Christ says: come ye blessed. To the others: Depart from me. Or so it is said.

In El Salvador, the *guardia* peer out from behind the smoked windows of vans, like Mississippi sheriffs behind their shades: the look of a leveled gun.

In Nicaragua, the guns have learned to smile. Like cornucopias of steel, they whisper promises: Dear children, trust us. From our barrels pour the ABC's, medicines, a blessed life. Trust us, stroke us, vote for us. In our dark void is concealed all your future.

DB

"The one who pleases God is greatly loved. The memory of the wicked will perish" (3:1–4:20)

3:1–9 What a change of tone emerges, a celebration. A Beethovian hymn to joy!

And as always, the pretension and near prevailing of death is deflated and denied.

"Torment" . . . "affliction" . . . "destruction"—such was the lot of the martyrs. Now, the horrors they underwent are told once more: but only to banish, to declare the sufferings rendered null and void—the death of death!

A kind of "insanity" ruled, for awhile: it "judged them dead," the dossiers of the just closed, once for all.

✦ ✦ ✦

Only wait. What was closed is—disclosed. The word of God reopens the case, scrutinizes the dossier anew, proceeds in judgment against the judges.

Thus another declaration: life speaks the last word. Our God is God of the living. The just are at length vindicated. They dwell in "the hand of God. They dwell "in peace."

✦ ✦ ✦

3:4 A word unique in the Hebrew bible, to this occasion, this celebration: "immortality." Let us linger over it, savor the certainty, the outcome:

"If in human eyes—"

(surely not any humans, not the more or less guilty bystanders—but the persecutors, guards, police, torturers, surveillers, disappearers, jailers, judges, executioners)—

"if in the eyes of these, the just receive a deserved punishment, yet their hope is brimming with immortality."

"Hope, brimming." The hope that hopes on, the "hope against hope" summoned by Paul. Hope prevailing despite all, hope lodged firm in a promise never renounced or canceled.

Another wisdom poet knew of this hope "in despite," and celebrated it:

With God
at my right hand
I shall not be shaken . . .

My heart is glad
and my soul rejoices,

my body too
abides in confidence:

because
You will not abandon my soul
to the nether world,
nor will You suffer
Your faithful one
to undergo corruption.

You will show me
the path of life,

fullness of joy
in Your presence,

delight
at Your right hand
forever! (Psalm 16:8–11)

✦ ✦ ✦

3:5 A chastisement in this world, followed by immeasurable glory. Thus does the word of God place the vocation of humans in a divine perspective.

Suffering is monstrous in prospect and befalling. And in retrospect is a mere nothing.

✦ ✦ ✦

This side of death, in knowledge that death impends—in the soul of Jesus an uncontainable emotion wells up:

> Jesus went down on his knees and prayed in these words: "Father, if it be your will, take this cup from me: yet not my will but yours be done . . ."
>
> In his anguish he prayed with all the greater intensity, and his sweat became like drops of blood falling to the ground . . . (Luke 22:41–42, 44)

We think also of Paul. Amid setback and scorn, how tranquil he abides! His demeanor sets to naught the awful present, the no less awful prospect of suffering to come. Neither is to the point:

> I consider
> the sufferings
> of the present
> to be nothing,
> compared
>
> with the glory
> to be revealed
> in us (Romans 8:18)

One trembles in face of such fortitude. Did Paul fear nothing? Did he know of the fear that started in the Savior a sweat of blood? Did Paul fear for his lack of fear?

✦ ✦ ✦

Two scenes open here, two modes of judgment, two geographies of time and place. The one is earthbound, a kangaroo court, sordid, ridden with self-interest, morally incoherent, in pursuit of legalized murder. And lording it over the woeful proceedings, over judge and hangman, is—the "envious devil."

The second scene, occurring within the first yet wonderfully transcending it, is the provenance of the word of God: the piercing glance of the Spirit, and meaning lent to dark matters.

The truth is at hand, the radical correction of the text of this "Justice System" of the Realm of Necessity—timebound, earthbound as this is "bound to be."

But by no means final. Final is this:

"God tried the just, and found them worthy."

This is indeed horrendous—that God admits—no, glories in having part in—murder. Part, great part or small.

Does God stay his hand?

✦   ✦   ✦

This God of non-intervention. Indeed the saints cry out: given such a God, does the course of the world proceed even more horrendously?

We are in the realm of faith, we are told: of the psalmist, of Job, of Jesus. But no matter who, no matter the dignity, the moral stature. God will not be held answerable. We search the great texts: they look back at us, the look of a lion who kills, or who does not.

Or a sphinx. But in any case, silence.

✦   ✦   ✦

The "testing" is a kind of noble biblical commonplace (if the word be apt), neither demeaning nor frivolous.

> You have tested us,
> O God
>
> You have tried us,
>
> as silver is tried
> by fire (Psalm 66:10)

✦   ✦   ✦

> God speaks to Job:
> "Would you refuse
> to acknowledge
> My right?
>
> Would you
> condemn Me
>
> that you
> may be justified?"

And of Jesus we read: "A strong cry and tears." "If it be possible, let this cup pass." It was not possible. So "a sweat of blood."

And the like testimony is uttered by Paul, and included in his instruction to the faithful. Let them take it as a matter of fact: the "testing" will come, harsh—a commonplace Christian event.

Paul writes with a kind of clinical detachment. The blow falls hard indeed. But afterward comes maturity, which brings surcease, even to bitter events:

> Since
> it is the Lord
> who judges us,
>
> He chastens us,
> to keep us
> from being condemned
>
> with the rest
> of the world (1 Corinthians 11:32)

One recoils at the imagery, thinking that it does the community small honor. Is life to be construed as a kind of Dickensian school, and we as adolescents, restless and unruly? Shall we feel the thwack of a ferule from on high?

> God
> (disciplines us)
> for our true profit,
>
> that we may share
> God's holiness.
>
> At the time
> it is administered,
> discipline
>
> seems a cause
> for grief and not for joy.
> But later,
> it brings
> the fruit
> of peace and justice
>
> to those
> trained in its school (Hebrews 12:10–11)

✦ ✦ ✦

3:8 "The just will judge the nations and rule over many peoples . . ." As verified also by Paul:

> "Do you not know
> that believers
> will judge the world . . . ?" (1 Corinthians 6:2)

The flat statement invites a pause, and pondering. Wisdom is turning the world's wisdom on its head.

✦   ✦   ✦

Wisdom sends the infinitely rich and powerful One forth
as poor and helpless, in His mission of inexpressible mercy,
to die for us on the cross . . .

The shadows fall. The stars appear. The birds fall to sleep.
Night embraces the silent half of the earth. A vagrant,
a destitute wanderer with dusty feet, finds his way down a
new road.

A homeless God, lost in the night, without papers, without
identification, without even a number, a frail expendable
exile lies down in desolation under the sweet stars of the
world and entrusts Himself to sleep.

("Hagia Sophia," Thomas Merton)

✦   ✦   ✦

The saints and martyrs, those "frail expendable" ones, are these to
judge the judges, the great ones who wrought their destruction? Can a
more artful, ironic turning of the tables be imagined? Or for that matter,
a more unlikely?

Imagine it then. Along these lines perhaps: judgment is the task and
vocation of believers and in no unspecified "end time," but here and now.

The community accepts this as a working principle: the powers of this
world are radically incapable of judging one another, of setting ethical
norms of behavior binding on all.

Nothing of this. Instead, a far different rule. This: the greater power
seized, the less accountability conceded.

Thus an image of the world emerges, a subhuman image: a bear pit, a
bombing run, an abattoir, a morgue. The powerful, intent on keeping or
enhancing their status, their world markets and military advantage, circle
one another, spy on one another, assess points of advantage or weakness.

And when judged expedient (the code word is *just*), there occurs a bloody
fracas known as war (or an unbloody one known as "sanctions"), accompanied by a round of air assaults, aimed indiscriminately at the innocent,
the children and aged and ill.

And afterward, a sibyl of violent intent offers a justification for the
savagery. Her words are vile, and shame our ears: "We think they (the
sanctions against Iraq) are worth the price." Manifestly worth it, since her
bombers, her tacticians, rather than paying the "price," exact it.

✦   ✦   ✦

The following litany of loss and death is worthy of pondering: Since 1945, the United States has bombed China, Korea, Guatemala, Indonesia, Cuba, Congo, Peru, Vietnam, Laos, Cambodia, Grenada, Lebanon, Libya, El Salvador, Nicaragua, Panama, Iraq (as of this writing, ongoing), Kuwait, Bosnia, Sudan, Afghanistan, Yugoslavia. (Pakistan, Albania, Macedonia, and Bulgaria were bombed, but by mistake).

✦   ✦   ✦

Who then is to cry murder most foul, to call the murderers to account? Wisdom answers: "the just." Isaiah: "My servant." Paul: "the believers."

Let the Church cry out, someone, or some few believers. Or perhaps even many!

✦   ✦   ✦

3:9 No wonder the name of the book, *Wisdom*. Each verse encapsulates so perfect a pearl.

Daring too, as here:

> Those
> who place confidence
> in God,
>
> will attain the truth.

As also in Proverbs 28:5:

> Those
> who seek God
> understand all.

We are in the realm of a great surmise, a great promise.

There is in all visible things an invisible fecundity, a dimmed light, a meek namelessness, a hidden wholeness. This mysterious Unity and Integrity is Wisdom, the Mother of all, *Natura naturans*.

> There is in all things an inexhaustible sweetness and purity, a silence that is a fount of action and joy. It rises up in wordless gentleness and flows out to me from the unseen roots of all created being, welcoming me tenderly, saluting me with indescribable humility.
>
> This is at once my own being—my own nature, and the Gift of my Creator's Thought and Art within me, speaking as Hagia Sophia, speaking as my sister, Wisdom.
>
> ("Hagia Sophia," Thomas Merton)

✦ ✦ ✦

We see the promise verified—and with manifest irony.

That turning of the tables again! The truth tellers are the "unlikely ones." They dwell in the shadows: a purblind world neither esteems nor honors them. Yet the truth is theirs. Despised, ignored, they offer the world a peerless gift, access to the truth. Perhaps the only access the world can lay claim to.

What do we love in them, why do we seek them out? They have no ax to grind, no ideology to block the clear flow.

✦ ✦ ✦

A few Jesuits attain this candor, this simplicity of heart. One such is Stephen Kelly of my community. Yet once more, as I set down these reflections, he is a prisoner. Quite simply, he refuses to be silenced or neutered by the powers, intent as they are on bombing and betrayal, on waging war and multiplying suffering, on sowing the earth with the poison of depleted uranium.

Kelly, his soul far reaching and acute, says his NO.

He and his like offer a precious truth, the price and reward of courage. Punished as they are, abiding in peace where they choose to be, in court and prison, they enable us as well. Because our friend has chosen to pay a price, we grow more thoughtful, we take heart. We walk the earth with less shame.

✦ ✦ ✦

The gentle wisdom of verse 9:

> . . . the faithful
> shall abide with God
> in love.

The words are jewels in a ring of gold.

They gleams with a deliberate, rich ambiguity. The faithful shall abide either "in God's love for us," or "in our love for God."

And yet another sense is implied:

> those
> who are faithful
>
> in their love
> for God,
>
> shall abide
> with God.

Or yet again:

> those
> who are faithful
>
> to the love
> God has for them,
>
> shall . . .

Each version is true, each a facet of a precious truth. We are invited to turn the saying about in the light, in admiration and awe.

One notes a double aspect of the Vision promised—and this in a single verse. Beatitude will include the fullness of truth and the open heart of love.

And with tentative, untidy steps, and many a backward glance, we go on our way.

✦ ✦ ✦

3:11–12 Wisdom is joined to "discipline," and much is made in our book of the connection. The word recurs again and again: the just honor discipline (Hebrew: *musar*), the wicked despise and spurn it.

Musar hums with resonance, hinting at a lexicon of moral maturity— and the way to this as well: paying attention, mindfulness, submitting to correction, education of mind and heart, enlightened behavior.

✦ ✦ ✦

"Vain is the hope of such as these." Those who neglect discipline throttle the austere summons of "hope against hope." In its place, we note an apish optimism based on a favoring culture, income, job, gender, prevailing ego or the like.

✦ ✦ ✦

Christ, for his part, will have nothing of this aping of the world's ways. Let a hyperbole embody the teaching:

> What profit would one show, were he to gain the whole world and destroy himself in the process?
>
> What can one offer in exchange for his very self? (Matthew 16:26)

✦ ✦ ✦

Paul echoes the vanity. "Dwellers on the earth" lay claim to the Christian community as well. The prevailing culture would have believers swamped by the goods of this world. But the truth issues a contrary call, and a warning:

If our hopes in Christ are limited to this life only, we are the most
pitiable of humans (1 Corinthians 15:19)

✦   ✦   ✦

We sense it, a perfume rises from the page. Paul knows goodness and
glory. His pen dwells like the brush of a master on the vivid joys of the
blessed:

> Eye
> has not seen,
> nor ear heard,
>
> nor has it entered
> the mind to know,
>
> what God has prepared
> for those who love. . . .

The author of Wisdom is no gull: he knows evil as well. Abruptly, shockingly, he dips a quill in bile. His words are like wounds dealt—the wicked
are cut down:

> vain
> is their hope,
>
> fruitless
> their labors,
>
> worthless
> their works! (3:11)

It is as though fury overmastered him, a Daniel come to judgment.
He sets down a second triad of damnation:

> their wives
> are foolish,
>
> their children
> depraved,
>
> accursed
> their posterity! (3:12)

What shall we name the tirade?

The spontaneous combustion of a culture of verbal pyrotechnics, brute energy, down putting, bullying, insult, dudgeon, jousting.

The culture of Job and his bombastic friends echoes here. A culture that blesses and curses with equal abandon, now soothing, now striking out in fury.

And what of God? Shall Jawe endorse the words? So it is said: the curse is God's own word.

And we are appalled, we, children of a tamer God.

✦   ✦   ✦

4:1 In the era of Wisdom, we are told that immortality is a large issue. A question arises: is the issue native to the Hebrew faith, or is it a Greek borrowing?

It would seem the latter, as will appear.

✦   ✦   ✦

A puzzling start:

> Better
> is childlessness
> with virtue,
>
> for immortal
> is its memory.

A double entendre, one thinks. Immortality is summoned in two ways: as persistent human memory, and as promise.

Memory persists, and more: it invites imitation. We summon the memory of the great, and from them we receive a meed of exemplary virtue, holiness, compassion. The gifts pour out and out: they go by many names, each fragrant and enticing. Memory enables, the saints and martyrs lead us on.

And the promise, what of that? Among Christians, immortality is not included in the divine promise. Resurrection is: another matter entirely, implying acceptance of a harsh prelude—death.

✦ ✦ ✦

4:2

> When it is present,
> all imitate it;
> when absent,
> they long for it.

The reference ("it") is manifestly "immortality."

Suspect. We are in the realm, the inflated realm, of empire. There, a cultural supposition affects (or perhaps infects, or afflicts) all. It must be resisted, a monstrous hypothesis.

This: social, political, economic systems (yes, and religion as well) dwell in plenitude—they are ultimate, the last, highest, best word of human achievement. I that sense, immortal. We are in pharaonic time: the "systems" will know (indeed will tolerate) no replacement. No Moses. There exist no alternatives, no other way of organizing, vindicating, honoring human life.

✦ ✦ ✦

The cultural supposition implies a threat, and is inevitably backed by an immense military apparatus. Thus, war and preparation for war become a staple of empire: it embodies the supposition as well as pushing its sure proof. We, comprising the imperialist entity, are immortal.

✦ ✦ ✦

To speak of America, immortal urges do not come cheap, whether in lives or resources. Suppositions of immortality must be dramatized by threat and act. So, death is dealt abroad: from Germany to Japan to Vietnam to Central America to Iraq to Bosnia to Kosovo, and on and on.

(Over the period of time required to set down these reflections, one cannot but note how the litany of woe and crime, grows and grows).

And the carnage, the ecological chaos, touch nothing of the favored claque, the leaders of the empire. Death is invariably dealt elsewhere. Under a vast military cope, the privileged rejoice in their entitlement: in progeny and promise, they (we) are citizens of an immortal system. Or so it is believed, and dramatized with manifest confidence. The price of imperial immortality: many must die.

✦ ✦ ✦

In the text before us, Greek imagery is notable. In the palaestra, athletes compete: one wins and is crowned with a laurel. And a cortege of honor forms. An image of beatitude, and the triumph of the crowned believer.

Paul frequently summoned the analogy: Christians also compete for a prize. One example will suffice:

> You know that while all the runners in the stadium take part in the race, the award goes to one.
>
> In that case, run so as to win!
>
> Athletes deny themselves all sorts of things. They do this to win a crown of leaves that withers, but we to win a crown that is imperishable (1 Corinthians 9:24–25)

And so on. Whether one finds the imagery persuasive is perhaps another matter. Or whether Christianity is aptly described here also might raise questions. Is the faith a contest whose outcome postulates a single winner, or even a winning team, with many losers trailing behind? And what is the fate of those "also rans"?

✦ ✦ ✦

More befitting our subject, one thinks, is an exhortation of Jesus, lucid and oneiric, to the church in Smyrna:

> Be faithful unto death, and I will give you the crown of life (Revelation 2:10)

Here the promise is coherent, social, and, in the highest sense, orthodox. No winners-losers, no "imperishable crown" of immortality, no imagery borrowed from an imperial game of winners-losers. And most important of all (and in conflict with imperial behavior), no death inflicted on others: instead, death accepted. In the image of Christ, death undergone.

The Savior in sum commends to the believing community his own behavior, his undergoing and submission. A Christian "credo" in small compass.

✦ ✦ ✦

4:3 We are offered a "Parable of the Prolific Posterity of the Wicked." Our author's engagement (and more, his enragement!) is in full cry.

We pause over the text, bemused. Uncomfortable too, perhaps, conscious that at some stage of genetics, one may well have descended from a wicked ancestor. Therefore are the descendants condemned, root and branch?

✦ ✦ ✦

Why indeed this superfluity of bile, poured out against a (presumed) unborn—also a (presumed) innocent? Is the old canard here resuscitated,

the sins of the fathers visited on the progeny? One presumed that the prophets had disposed of the dank notion once for all.

It would seem otherwise. Here, one thinks, wisdom fails the wise.

+ + +

(BJ offers not a demurring word in regard to this puzzling atavism.
Reference is made in passing to a parable of Jesus, the sower and his seed.
But no word of the marked difference between our Wisdom text and the
Lucan parable. The difference is worth noting, however. The subject of the
parable is the immediate fate of seed as it leaves the hand of the sower
and falls to ground. There are unhappy episodes, seeds die and die. But
the ending is totally at odds with the present text of Wisdom. The story of
Jesus is all of hope. Some seed "fell on good soil, grew, and yielded grain a
hundredfold" [8:8]. Then the contrast: the stark pessimism of Wisdom's
(sic) conclusion: Children born of lawless unions give evidence, when God
judges them, of the wickedness of their parents.

Awful.)

+ + +

4:7–14 Onto more solid ground.

Wisdom recovers and grows surpassingly wise: the seer engages a difficult question, and directly. What to make of the early death of the just?
And even more thornier. What make of the God who thus decrees?

We touch here on one aspect of the large question that tormented Job.
Suffering and injustice flog the world to knee: the just suffer, the wicked
ride high. And what are believers to make of the tragic reversal of ethical
expectation? And what make of this chameleon God, maker and unmaker,
author and model of roles, protagonist and antagonist, defender and pros-
ecutor, prevailing promethean and holy sufferer—all these in bewildering
array?

+ + +

The scene is great Alexandria, that radiant haven of the intellect. The
Jews in dispersion are cosmopolites, strenuous in maintaining points of
contact between Greek culture and their own tradition.

Human immortality, its proofs devised by Plato, is much in the air. The
soul is immortal by nature and destiny: a magnificent insight—and a gift
to our Hebrew author.

We take note: to the believing Jews, platonic proofs are in the nature of
an influence, rather than a methodology adopted. Philosophy, even the
most elevated, holds small interest for the author of Wisdom. His method
is in sharp contrast with the Greek: he is simple, almost childlike. With no

preamble he announces a sublime truth, a conclusion drawn. And not a single proof.

He is certain that his insight does not issue from the mind's native labors, its task of searching out premise and conclusion. No mighty intellect he, wrestling for an angel's secret. No: he is simply the amanuensis of a word he did not initiate. A truth has been revealed, he is deputed to transmit it.

✦ ✦ ✦

Heretofore in Jewish wisdom literature, existence after death was imagined as larval, perpetual—and dour beyond imagining. Humans were consigned to a kind of crepuscular twilight, or a predawn: in an uninviting ambiance, the dead might be said to exist, but barely.

Exist? The word honors the fate of an amorphous ghost, shadow of a former self, one who in another world was composed of solid flesh and precious blood.

✦ ✦ ✦

Here a problem arises. What of the many among the just who die young, by whatever dire disease, mischance, martyrdom? Will their virtue, to all intents brought to naught, be duly rewarded?

The answer: elsewhere, elsewhen, and by the power of God.

For a start, the revelation is eminently commonsensical. It is not length of days that brings honor: as old age approaches, a hundred ways of decline afflict or threaten. Some are abrupt, some all but imperceptible.

How grow old gracefully? One has choices. (The present commentator, may one interject, has experimented widely).

He (I) may choose to grow grumpy, petrified, vacuous, turgid, banal, despotic—or some awful, artful variation on the above.

In sum, one may become the "Nobodaddy" (the "father of nothing") caricatured by William Blake.

Then, thanks be, other, better choices are at hand. "Intelligence" and "an unsullied life"—these are the hallmarks, the attainments possible to the aged: and by implication, to those of any age—old, young, middling.

And a warning. Stupid and defiled, the world as such stands "over against" such attainment. In the Alexandrian era, we have noted how the faithful were threatened by assimilation, betrayal, religious indifference, the notorious skepticism of the Greeks.

How conduct one's life in such circumstance? The faithful are called to remake the world, their world. They know the truth, the talk. Let them walk it steadfastly, the way of holy tradition.

No matter one's sum of years: be steadfast. The essentials are temple and torah. Do not forget; forgetting is death before death. Through mindfulness, "intelligence," one gathers, preserves, distills the herbs of memory into a heady Chartreuse.

✦ ✦ ✦

And today? Let one welcome like gifts and esteem them: mindfulness, intelligence, discernment. The essentials of the tradition are prayer, sacrament, community. These enable, amid a culture unimaginably defiled.

✦ ✦ ✦

Now, to the puzzle of that just youth who died—prematurely, as is judged.

The judgment, let it be confessed, leans on assumptions proper to the world, not to the faithful. Consider the story of Enoch (Genesis 5:24), who "walked with God," a phrase that implies, not death, but a bodily raising from time and this world. Or the story of Elijah, who "went up to heaven in a whirlwind" (2 Kings 2:11).

Thus the youth summoned here. He was surrounded by the stupidity and sin of a world which owes nothing, knows nothing of his passionate resolve—to know and serve God.

That world would have him for its own, its votary. To degrade intelligence with malice, and purity with perfidy.

But God has other plans: the youthful just one is "transported."

✦ ✦ ✦

4:12–13 An interjection. And ever so subtly the theological treatise becomes a homily. Let those of whatever age know: "intelligence" and the "unsullied life" are threatened. And the threat is especially grave, it is implied, against the young. For the witchery of paltry things obscures what is right, and the whirl of desire transforms the innocent mind.

✦ ✦ ✦

The revelation is famously seized on and ensconced in Christian liturgies, a midrash celebrating youthful saints:

> She grew perfect
> in a brief span,
>
> came quickly
> to plenitude.
>
> Her soul
> was pleasing to God,
>
> who sped her
> from the midst of wickedness.

Always, we note, clear moral boundaries are set, a strong sense of apartness is honored, even insisted on.

Shall we conclude that a siege mentality is commended, lines drawn, the wicked identified beyond doubt, and the "chosen" also?

No. Our chronicler of Wisdom shows a more nuanced, complex face. Since Jews dwell in a realm of honored intelligence, let them pay due tribute, let civilized converse clarify both difference and likeness. Let minds engage minds in a dance, a skill heady as the mingling of noble vintages.

Let the Jews be conscious of the gifts they bring—memory, tradition, symbols long tried in fires of tribulation, deeds of liberation celebrated in song and drama.

✦ ✦ ✦

And the people of faith are urged to venture further: for what is wisdom without the questioning of wisdom?

Thus. Philosophy, drama, poetry, architecture, sculpture, the deep wells of Greek genius: and two buckets lowered in the well, Greek and Jewish. Are these rival vessels, and unrelated?

And apart from Hebrew wisdom, summed up on knowledge of God—do these suffice for a plenary humanism?

Or is not Greek genius lacking in just this: "memories of saving intervention, of deeds of liberation"?

Indeed, do Greeks, as well as Jews, not require liberating?

Thus the Jewish genius: to raise such questions, avidly, audaciously.

✦ ✦ ✦

Another question: what, Greek friends, think you of this? We and our prophets announce a God of compassion, God of "widows and orphans," "aliens, strangers." Without a "breakthrough from above" in favor of the victims and the powerless, does not even a renowned democracy risk becoming cramped and despotic, or banal, self-serving?

✦ ✦ ✦

4:14–19 In a subtle interplay of contrast and analogy, the argument continues.

The "crowds," the "people," are equated here with the "impious."

Puzzled, we will let the synonyms stand for the moment. One fact seems clear. The author is neglecting, or ignoring Greek finesse.

In a golden age of philosophy, our text speaks of neither Plato nor Aristotle. Likewise, of the great dramatists not a word.

Not that the inquiry lacks drama or its apron stage. At the city gates, in the synagogue this people are wont to hammer out their questions: the law, the meaning of Scripture, the activity of God in the world, their place in the scheme of things. (And be it noted too, our author is a Hebrew, a child of scorn, skilled in vituperation, his tongue honed on rabbinical argument).

✦   ✦   ✦

In accord with the injunction of Genesis, he "names things": and glories in naming them right. Glories—even when he is wrong.

Thus the equation "crowd-people-wicked" becomes a kind of code, a puzzle, a Zen hyphen. Let it venture out and out: cast into the waters, let it drift with the tides and winds of time. Let it land among faithful or renegade Jews or Greeks—a message in a bottle. Let each retrieve, uncork, sip. Make of it what one will!

In his own mind, the seer is sure. (He has also preserved his cover). The expressions, "crowd, people, wicked"—are meant to touch a nerve. They cut across class and status: they indict the willfully ignorant, wherever found.

The faithful Jews will know: they are not intended or indicted.

The renegades? Let them read as they run.

The Greeks? Let them, including the greatest among them, know this: they are not exempt from the ignorance that lurks beneath mask and buskin, in agora and demos.

Summon Job. Can the world's enigma, to the native powers of Jew or Greek all but opaque—can this torment be relieved, short of faith in God?

Eminence has its price. Some run without reading, inattentive, otherwise busied. What do they remain ignorant of—and the more culpable for their ignorance?

> That the elect of God
> find grace
> and mercy,
>
> and the saints,
> protection.

Ignorant, and culpable for ignorance of this truth: judgment is underway, in this time, in this world. Thus our wise author seeks (and finds) a better meaning for time than that of bland, blank duration or a cold conjunction of stars.

This is the essence of time: judgment is underway. And the judges? All unexpectedly, a theme revisited: they are the noble, youthful dead.

The reproving irony is set in place, neatly as a feather woven in a wing (verse 16):

Yes,
the just dead

condemn
the sinful living:

youth,
swiftly brought to closure

condemns

the many years
of the wicked aged.

✦ ✦ ✦

This sage must be sure of himself, one thinks, sure of his revelation.

He names his opponents—"the crowd," equated with "the wicked"—heaping on them large scorn.

His naming them (the renegades, one thinks) is like a wound opened. And he proceeds to rub the wound raw. Willful ignorance is their hallmark. To the wise, and to God, they are known—for knowing nothing.

The death of the just is a testing ground: and not solely for the just. How easily they are disposed of: a bullet, a rope, a deft blow—and a corpse.

And from such a scene, no one walks away unchanged. The terrible moment destroys vulnerable flesh. It also tests to the bone all involved: judges, executioners, more or less guilty bystanders, the faithful and the faithless.

✦ ✦ ✦

How awful to amend the above: but amended it must be.

For some walk away unchanged, even as they witnessed the crime—uncomprehending, declaiming in their hearts: we have seen nothing!

We have here a terrifying theology of refusal. And our wise one reserves his bleakest judgment—for the apostates. Amid the ferment of compatriot and Greek, of faith seeking intelligence, of intellect at the verge of faith—these are a dough dead on the tongue.

They are guilty bystanders—of life itself: and of death. They bring nothing to a wrenching bloodletting, they walk away with—nothing. So they live on, empty-handed, empty of soul, of merit and mind. They belong to no one, neither to Jew nor Greek.

They have renounced the truth, violated the life of the mind. They merit only scorn, the derisive laugh of God.

Death overtakes them before their death. Thus the urgency: death "right away." Thus an imagery of corpses unburied, the worst nightmare of the living.

In life no recourse: in death no relief—not even the relief of extinction. (Let alone the reward of the just and faithful, beatitude). For these turn-coats, Sheol's worst torment is reserved: derision and mockery from their like, those pale shades of demiexistence.

✦ ✦ ✦

The images are relentlessly vindictive. It is as though God were play-ing a double role: first, as judge, then a kind of eldritch gravedigger,

" . . . plunging them, speechless, precipitous, head first . . ." into oblivion.

Clods above, hell below. Their graves are unmarked: not a wisp of memory rises from the clay. Except this: an account of conscience, duly rendered. Execration, opprobrium.

The Digger spits on his hands, shovels them under. Then he walks away, a distasteful job done.

✦ ✦ ✦

We think of mercy, and of mercilessness. Of a judgment that takes both in account.

For ourselves, accountability is insisted on.

And what of God? Is the Deity also to be held accountable?

Job heard it, that word from the whirlwind: you, Job, I hold account-able. But do not dare hold Me accountable. In effect: you are not God. I am God.

✦ ✦ ✦

We ponder the merciless author, and his stigma laid on the flesh of the "wicked."

Who are these, the irredeemable?

And who as well, the incorruptibles, the "just," standing in pure light unshadowed?

We are puzzled, set off-kilter. Is it not true that among the living, shadow and light intermingle, virtue and deviance, goodness and sin? Ourselves trudging along, our hope reduced to this—the trudge itself, our need of ever new starts, our setbacks, dead ends, detours?

And how translate that awful name, "the renegades"?

✦ ✦ ✦

I venture something like this: institutions, systems, their sponsors: world class CEOs, supreme court judges, presidents, secretaries of defense, of state, of—etc., etc.,—these by implication are referred to. Whoever chooses to crush, denigrate, make sport of, deny bread or medicine or dwelling, punish, lock up, even remove from life, other humans.

More. Those who abandon the human circle. Who, acting anonymously,
safe in a maze of subalterns, "paperwork" and jargon, betray the social
compact, the "Yes" of humanist and/or religious consensus, the immemorial taken-for-granted of decent implication and follow through.

This implication: that the powerful are responsible for the powerless.
That hands are meant for service rather than withholding, hoarding, or
punishing. That jails are a savage folly, and death rows a celebration of
blood lust. These the just abominate.

chapter three

"What did pride avail? . . . All passed like a fleeing rumor . . . But the just live forever" (5:1–23)

5:1–5 From the world, a demented inn, from public insanity, we have come—to a scene of judgment, accountability.

But conventional "justice systems," with their witless baggage of forensic argument, omniscient judges, images of a blindfolded Dame, scales held aloft, punishment in the offing, the great pillared halls incised with "Equal Justice Under Law"—this pretense and straight-faced folly does no honor to civilization, let alone to this scriptural scene.

✦ ✦ ✦

No doubt the imagery of chapter 5 places us in a courtroom. But there are strong hints that the hideous "justice systems" of the world have been superceded. The text indicates a far different reality: a Council of Reconciliation.

Here, criminals, once Olympian, once "above the law," are hardly to be thought above justice.

But this is a peculiar justice. It aims at the healing of both sides: victims, their wounds and wounding memories: victimizers, their deformed humanity.

✦ ✦ ✦

Once, night ridden minds and hands ruled the world. They devised and wrought maltreatment of the just. Now at long last, such come to true understanding, to public confession of crime. Their hands relinquish tawdry, punishing credentials.

This "last judgment" proceeds with heavy emphasis on remorse—and, one thinks, an implied rehabilitation of the wicked.

✦ ✦ ✦

For ourselves, the scene is wonderfully restoring. Hope is in the air—even in the thin Himalayan air of a cosmic courtroom.

And we dare ask: can there be hope also for those monstrous

hangmen, the Eichmanns crouched in the well of the court, the shahs and juntas and supreme justices and Secretaries of Kafkaesque Bureaus of Necessary Killing?

Yes. For the scene implies a turning of tables, and more: a toppling of thrones.

✦   ✦   ✦

Among the Greeks, let us think Greek.

We raise a question: may it invite a creative mimesis. Does this scene of Wisdom impact on realities of today?

The scene, one thinks, resembles uncannily a trial of the Plowshares and other conscientious spirits.

We have seen such trials, their drastic, adroit turnaround of roles, a rehearsal of this scriptural rehearsal of judgment.

The accused—are they not shortly criminalized and convicted? Undoubtedly they are.

But wait, a notable reversal is at hand. It is as though the defendants donned judicial robes, hefted the gavel, assumed new, unprecedented roles. Now they act as prosecutors and judges—of the prosecutors and judges.

And the "law of the land," that dark instrument of crime—at long last those who wield it are unmasked: their weapon is broken in pieces, reduced to grist for the mills of the gods.

✦   ✦   ✦

What to say of that notorious law? It is both lethal and—legal. It is a loaded gun, registered, approved, fully licensed. It rests in authorized hands, its barrel held to the heads of multitudes: and the standoff has lasted for more than fifty years. Authorities have perfected the weapon, burnished it, brandished it about the world.

Its name is atomic bomb: and more recently, depleted uranium weaponry. Both have been discharged, a salutary lesson to the world. Multitudes have perished, the innocent, the aged, the unborn, from Hiroshima to Kosovo.

And what of those who devised the weaponry, deployed, discharged it?

Of these, not one was held accountable. The law of the land exempted them.

After Hiroshima the weapon flourished, copulated with its kind, multiplied—always in secret. Its sponsors and researchers and justifiers likewise flourished, copulated with their kind, died, were replaced by others who likewise etc., etc.

✦ ✦ ✦

At length, in courtrooms, whether in Pennsylvania, Maine, North Carolina, Maryland, Connecticut, Colorado—and in England and Scotland and Germany and Australia, within a hair's breadth, a minisecond of "too little, too late," Plowshares defendants went on trial. And a rehearsal opened of a "final judgment."

Surprises were in store: in such scenes they always are.

At long last, responsibility comes to bear. One hears it, in the hum and whirr, the sparks flying, the edge of the future honed on an emery wheel of conscience.

The daring-do is breathtaking. The defendants utter their "'J' accuse!" Did they perform the act of which they stand accused? They did, it is freely admitted. Conscience, common sense forced their hand. The government, not they, is guilty, and the armed forces: guilty of crimes against humanity, of developing and discharging weapons of indiscriminate destruction.

The epiphany, alas, is brief. The presumption of these hardy spirits is shortly declared intolerable. Cease and desist or be found in contempt!

Nonetheless. In a modest way, the empery of death has been shaken. Even in hell, the truth has been spoken.

✦ ✦ ✦

Probably while time lasts, we will hear no such ruminations as lie stark and visible on this page of Wisdom.

The great ones, confounded, are hailed before the bar. They have betrayed, tortured, defamed, killed, and always with impunity. They died in their beds, panegyrics followed, monuments were raised to their honor.

How then a trial? Among the dead?

✦ ✦ ✦

We must summon analogies.

Time has run out. We are in a time out of time, the "final day," the "last day," by which we mean: no day known to mortals.

And we hear from mouths long deemed wicked, mouths of the accused defendants, an astonishing utterance. Words of confusion of spirit, of confession.

Words of conversion? A long susurration of regret, a choral ode of unrelieved woe.

And a question. If remorse comes too late to nullify the judgment impending, of what point recording the words of the guilty? Would such a page not dishonor Wisdom? Would it be more than the fiction of a venomous cynic?

To the honor, even the glory of Wisdom, this page lies before us, this outburst of misery and redemption.

How interpret it? Perhaps as this—a long outreach of mercy, plucking the hell bound from hell.

✦ ✦ ✦

Condemnation is near. The accusers stand, the martyrs. Their wounds are evidence irrefutable.

The accused also stand. The killers have died: they mount a mournful threnody of grace abhorred and crimes multiplied. The words are uttered by traitors to the family of faith, usurers, prevaricators, diseased souls. Wielding vast power, they have wantonly crushed and killed.

✦ ✦ ✦

5:6–9 Now they repent: they tell of conversion of heart:
"We have wandered far from the path of truth."
Their mortal lives were shrouded in darkness:
"The light of justice has not shone for us."
"The sun has not risen for us."
Then, a miracle. Meager and tardy as an arctic dawn, mercy reaches them. Through the wounds of their victims, light shines—even for them. Redemption is at hand.

✦ ✦ ✦

5:10–12 A triad of quite beautiful tropes illumines the scene. The accused wax poetic. Let us record their images.

A poet died, his name, he declared, was writ in water.

Something of the same image here. The prow of a ship cleaves the waves: the vessel goes on its way, the waters surge back. No trace of passage. So with lives bereft of goodness.

Or wings carry a bird aloft. The air parts and makes way, the bird speeds on. No trace of its passage.

The third. (And we have, by conjecture, a Greek image rather than a Hebrew, a tribute perhaps to the adopted culture.)

An arrow speeds from the bow. Air is cloven, then surges back on itself.

Does the arrow find its mark? It may or may not:
"No way of knowing the path it took."

✦ ✦ ✦

5:13 Then, the compunctious summary of the guilty. In effect:

Scarcely born,
we ceased to be.

No trace of virtue.
Perversity
has eaten us
alive.

Thus, finis. A conventicle of the dead, and a confession: at long last, wrongs are set right.

✦   ✦   ✦

5:14 How cunningly the fabric of narrative is woven.

Now for a moral commentary on the preceding: a triad of images, very Greek in their subtlety and fecundity. Call the verses "The Folly of Wicked Endeavor."

The same theme, more analogies!

And the fierce critic of the wicked has turned about: now he becomes their implicit advocate.

A hint is dropped: the truth of their conversion is underscored. As though to say, your images touched my heart. They flowered there. I bless them, I would add to them.

✦   ✦   ✦

And I would subtract from them as well! I counter your (and my) images of evanescence, with others, images of glory clashing with images of shame. A "Yes then, you were right."

And a curious phrase: "the hope of the wicked." Hope for what?—for an outcome more substantial—approval, permanence in possessions, peace amid turmoil, silencing of pangs of conscience?

In any case, avers the wise one, that hope is hopeless of attainment. You the wicked, have offered three images of No Outcome.

I give back four. That "hope" of yours is like "tumbleweed in the wind," like "foam tossed in a tempest," like "wind-driven smoke." And wonderfully apt, your hope is like "the memory of a nomad, camping here and there for a single day."

✦   ✦   ✦

5:15–17 Now for the true and substantial outcome.

You, the renegades—you disgrace the pages graced by the just. You dwell there in the text, your untruths made plain, your crimes laid bare. With good reason it is said: you exist only by virtue of your victims. Did you think to extinguish their memory? They live on, the very heartbeat of the human heart.

And you? Your self-chosen destination is—Sheol, your survival meager, bare, subterranean, in a garbage heap of creation.

✦ ✦ ✦

The just "live forever." The phrase encompasses a radiant, piercing beatitude, a community of saints and martyrs, ever present to the Presence. "Eye hath not seen, nor ear heard . . ."

And more: gently, suavely, with power, a personal gesture is offered. Symbols of transcendent glory are placed in heroic hands:

"Royal splendor, and a fair diadem from the Lord Himself."

The gesture is hardly an empty one. The once powerless, lifeless victims, fallen in a welter of blood—for them:

"all, all is changed:

a terrible beauty is born."

These are resurrected, these rule.

In the eternal now, theirs is God's "right hand." Theirs, God's "arm" of protection.

✦ ✦ ✦

Time for a poem, in honor of the Poet:

> They spoke to him in Hebrew and he understood
> them: in Latin and Italian and
> he understood them. Speech palled
> on them and they turned to the silence
> of their equations. But God listened to them
> as to a spider spinning its web
> from its entrails: the mind swinging
> to and fro over an abysm
> of blankness. They are speaking to me still,
> he decided, in the geometry
> I delight in, in the figures
> that beget more figures. I will answer
> them as of old with the infinity
> I feed on. If there were words once
> they could not understand. I will show
> them now space that is bounded
> but without end, time that is where
> they were or will be: the eternity
> that is here for me and for them
> there: the truth that with much labor
> is born with them and is to be
> sloughed off like some afterbirth of the spirit.

("Dialectic," *Collected Poems*, R. S. Thomas)

✦ ✦ ✦

5:18–24 Our author—a man given to moods, and to matching variety of skills! We have seen it before: his quill is dipped in gall, then in honey.

Now, he dips quill in another fluid, and sets down a furious text, a runnel of fire! An apocalypse writhes on the page. The end time, the end of the human affair, the end of wickedness.

And a vast combat, together with unexampled upheaval in nature—these burst before our eyes.

It is as though a monk, a wild-eyed visionary, had vanished in prayer and entered another world.

Returning, he set to work, crowding the pages of a Book of Kells with creatures never seen on land or sea. Gorgons and trolls and leviathans and behemoths!

Such images, we are told, are common to the apocalyptic genre—but hardly native to Wisdom literature.

Nonetheless, let those in search of wisdom know this: a battle is inevitable, and creation dissolving in chaos.

The transition is awesome. Abruptly we are tumbled from beatitude to horror. (And, as we have come to admire and now must fear—with what subtlety and skill.)

End time, with a vengeance: a battle, a tipping over of the table of creation.

✦ ✦ ✦

A standoff? God stands with the just, "covering them with his arm, as with a buckler," a shield, a military accoutrement. Then the battle, and a militant intervention of the deity, in allegorical detail. "Zeal for armor," and more: God ". . . shall arm creation to requite the enemy." "Justice for breastplate . . ." "Judgment for helmet." "Invincible holiness for shield" . . . "Invincible anger for whetted sword."

✦ ✦ ✦

The transition lunges forward, as though from crest to trough to crest in a single overwhelming wave. The combatants initially were: God versus the ungodly. Now the conflict widens: the entire creation joins the fray.

The image is awesome. War turns total. One by one, or all together, the powers of creation fall before the superhuman protagonists. The war is a template of all wars, World War Finis: its prey is every living being, including the unborn (but there will be no unborn). It is ecological, cosmic omnicide.

With perhaps two objectives. The first is willed: demise of the wicked.

The other, alas, is unwitting, but inevitable. The creation perishes in firestorm.

✦ ✦ ✦

This we know, if we know anything. Our own lifetime has seen the threat, carnivorous, appetitive for the flesh, blood, marrow of the created universe. The gun cocked. Ready, aim . . .

And all but loosed are the gods of Armageddon.

✦ ✦ ✦

Thus
lawlessness

shall lay the earth waste,

and evildoing
overturn

the thrones of potentates (5:23)

The summary is fearsome, artful, somewhat fretful. It signals a return of moral attention to the great ones who were urged at the start, to "Love justice, you who judge the earth!"

And a warning: let kings and judges know that wickedness in high places (their places!) pollutes the creation, threatens all the living, including themselves.

chapter four

"Honor Wisdom, you princes, that you may reign eternally" (6:1–25)

6:1–9 Lo! we are in the royal presence itself. An instruction is immanent, a warning and guideline. Needless to say, the message goes radically counter to the behavior of worldly authority.

As for the messenger, admitted to the king's presence—does he not know that bowing and scraping befit the occasion, the privilege?

It does not befit. No, he has a word to deliver, a message from One to whom indeed, awe is due. Due from the king as well as the messenger!

Let the instruction then be uttered forthrightly. Its strong, perhaps unwelcome import defines, even as it rejects, the pretensions of the powerful. Do these earthlings think themselves omnipotent? Denial of such presumption merits repeating. Let it be raised then, a din in royal ears! For the chief of state (of whatever state) is frequently distracted, sometimes even distraught. Contrary winds beat about a crowned head. Self-interest purrs away, counselors are like a pride of great cats prowling about the throne. They hunger for a share of the action—to his advantage, they insist. Then let his highness consent to give ear, to play god, master of life and death.

But this is a forbidden game. One alone gives life, the living God.

✦ ✦ ✦

If only he knew: the king too is ruled.

But suppose he ignores his bondage to ancestral pride and his own ambition, his bondage to those who counsel him wrongly—and suppose, in consequence, the messenger delivers no more than a dead letter—and knows it.

Still let this be proclaimed, and recorded:

> Authority
> was given you
> by God,
>
> and sovereignty
> by the most High

> who shall probe
> your works
>
> and scrutinize
> your counsels! (6:3)

✦   ✦   ✦

Momentous suppositions are at work here, like hidden piers of conscience. Chief among them, deepest laid, is instruction on the nature of sin. We take note of circumstance and setting. The word of God is conveyed without protocol or politesse, directly to headquarters.

Let the chiefs of whatever state take heed. They have been warned:

> For those in power,
> rigorous scrutiny impends.
>
> To you therefore,
> princes,
> are my words addressed,
>
> that you may learn wisdom,
> and may not sin (6:8–9)

✦   ✦   ✦

Then and now, the implication is momentous.

No such severe words, we note, are delivered, say, to a shantytown door, to a migrant farm workers' union office. No such warning to a welfare parent. Nor to the homeless. Nor to those who stand in a police lineup. Nor to those on death row. No such word for such. An entirely different word: a word of sovereign mercy.

But for the powerful, urgency unadorned:

> The lowly
>
> are pardoned
> out of mercy:
>
> but the mighty
>
> shall be mightily
> put to the test (6:6)

Thus the Wisdom of God. The passion of God for a just world.

Indignation and fury are barely contained in face of the appalling antics of leaders, their machinations of advantage and ego.

To the White House, let us say, arrives the messenger. To the loftiest of places, and the least accessible to a salutary word. There, by presumption, sin is imputed:

Because

> though you were ministers
> of God's realm,
>
> you judged not rightly,
> did not keep the law,
>
> nor walk in accord
> with the will of God (6:4)

✦ ✦ ✦

And one thinks—how apt! What of those "spiritual advisers" summoned in the winter of '99, presumably to loosen the knot from the president's throat?

Would these viziers be inclined to open the book of Wisdom chapter 6, to help this fellow arrive at a biblical knowledge of sin—his sin? Which is to say, not a word of our text lingers over matters of sexual deviance. Not a word.

Provocative, subversive—and dangerous. This messenger of Wisdom might well take care of his own life and limb! The sin he adduces is—pride of place.

The fantasy, full blown, dangerous, takes many forms. Mr. President, take warning. You, kings, shahs, juntas, prime ministers, secretaries of state, supreme court justices—you fancy yourselves masters of the world, you indulge fantasy and ignore consequence.

These are your sins. You prevaricate. You demean women. You manipulate the economy in favor of greed. You crush the poor of the land and the impoverished abroad, pledging as you do allegiance to multicorporate jackals. You wage awful wars. You kill, and twitch accountability away like an annoying insect. You enact hideous decrees, denying medicine and food where desperately needed, throttling innocent life through your wicked sanctions.

✦ ✦ ✦

The message is a moral instruction, never more needful than today. Sin is defined and imputed. Willful folly is here given habitation and name. Thus, according to the man of Wisdom, bespeaking the word of God. The word of a passionate God.

> . . . Often
> I think that there is no end
> to this torment and that the electricity
> that convulses us is the fire
> in which a god
> burns and is not consumed.

(*Collected Poems*, R. S. Thomas).

✦ ✦ ✦

6:10–11 How beautifully put, how adroit a master! Appeal is made to the best instincts of these rulers. No abstract morality is urged: nothing short of a compassionate exercise of power.

Then our man of Wisdom pronounces a blessing over those (rare) sovereigns who honor the Law and so attain wisdom:

> Those who holily
>
> keep guard
> over holy things,
>
> themselves
> shall be accounted
> holy.

✦ ✦ ✦

6:12–16 Our poet composes (perhaps better, improvises: one all but hears him ecstatically singing his paean)—a hymn to Wisdom, personified and feminine. She is

> resplendent
> and unfading,
>
> readily perceived
> by those
>
> who love Her,
>
> found
> by those
>
> who seek Her (6:12–13)

Foreshadowed here is a theology of grace, as Wisdom hastens to make Herself known, in anticipation of desire.

She is prevenient and urgent, pressing upon us the riches of God:

> The one
> who watches for Her
> at dawn
>
> shall not
> be disappointed:
>
> he shall find Her
> sitting at his gate. . . .
> The one
> who for her sake
>
> keeps vigil,

shall quickly
be free from care (6:14-15)

✦   ✦   ✦

We rejoice in her sovereign freedom, her mutuality and solicitude, her hunger for a return of love. Reversing culture and custom, daring, Wisdom ventures about in public, searching for a lover:

> She makes her rounds,
>
> seeking those
> worthy of her,
>
> graciously
> she presents herself
> in streets and squares.
>
> She has thought
> of them
>
> before they
> of her.

✦   ✦   ✦

Sophia is the mercy of God in us. She is the tenderness with which the infinitely mysterious power of pardon turns the darkness of our sins into the light of grace.

She is the inexhaustible fountain of kindness, and would almost seem to be in herself, all mercy.

So she does in us a greater work than that of creation: the work of new being in grace, the work of pardon, the work of transformation from brightness to brightness . . .

She is in us the yielding and tender counterpart of the power, justice and creative dynamism of the Father.

("Hagia Sophia," Thomas Merton)

✦   ✦   ✦

6:17-21 With a nimble mind and many strings to pluck, our poet is also a logician. Here, in favor of his beloved he composes a sorites, an "elliptical series of syllogisms."

Does the device seem dry, merely rhetorical? Be attentive, the text plays on the lyre of the heart, a delight:

> A sure beginning
>
> is a longing
> for her instruction.

Instruction leads to love.

Love implies
observance
of her law.

Her law
bestows
incorruptibility,

a very likeness
to God (6:17–18)

We marvel at the play of affection and discipline, of freedom and boundary. Wisdom engages mind and heart, draws both into her chorus.

And the conclusion is apt. Wisdom seizes on the prime symbols of power, "thrones and scepters" (6:21). She points to the one, raises the other on high for all to see, these trophies.

Do these, the seat of power and the golden ferule, please the regents? Let them take note of a greater Promise:

Honor Wisdom,
that you
may reign forever (6:21).

At first glance, the counsel wears a simple guise. It seems a light garment for a summery day of the mind, this urging to "honor Wisdom."

Then we reflect on the foregoing implications of such "honoring," as each is carefully spelled out. Harsh and close are the questionings of kings, and the command issued. Rulers of whatever clime or system— passionately give yourselves to works of justice and compassion.

What a weighty premise—and how rarely fulfilled!

✦   ✦   ✦

And on ourselves, plunged as we have been in a century of killerrulers, with small relief in sight—dark thoughts intrude, reminders of the killer-kings of the Bible and of our book of Wisdom as well, and its unrelenting counsel. Kings, take notice!

Need we recall? It was told that the mighty have hated the "needy just man": they resolved in concert (as though this were their communal urge throughout the ages):

Let us
oppress him . . .

let us
neither spare the widow
nor revere the old . . .

Our genius, poet and logician, presses on nonetheless. One senses that he knows well and bitterly: how small the chance that the mandate conveyed will be honored.

Small chance indeed—miniscule. Betrayal, lip service, guile, treachery, glib banality are the hallmarks of might.

Nevertheless! The truth must be uttered and handed on. The messenger is responsible for the message. He is not responsible for being heard.

Will a rare sovereign, or a few among the faithful, heed and obey?

Chances are, those who heed will be very scions and embodiments of irony. Wisdom enters a fallen world. There, like begets like, like is begotten of like: Wisdom is both mother and child of irony.

Let us be sanguine: one or a few will seek Wisdom, and pay up. That one, that few—they kneel before sovereign Reality, they honor Wisdom and vindicate the Godly, the human. And frequently, for this supremely offensive favor, they are struck down.

Does a king pledge honor to Wisdom? What large demands are implied in that embrace! He must renounce "the throne, the scepter." He is called to service, not domination.

Or is it the "needy just one" who embraces Her—has that one already taken Wisdom for a bride? For that let him be warned: he might well fall victim of—throne and scepter.

✦   ✦   ✦

Wisdom, as we have pondered her office in the world, is no gull, she is not taken in. She weighs, witnesses, judges. She is the compassion of God, but she is also God's justice. As such, hers is an indispensable office.

And here the irony: she lacks all credentials.

✦   ✦   ✦

For a moment, let us see the world as she does, stand where she stands. The world is a kind of courtroom: the time is a prelude to judgment.

Her Honor, Wisdom, enters. Let us imagine (the image cannot but be instructive) that before her stands the "needy just man" so repellant to the kings of earth.

He is accused of—God knows what. Any sort of charge will do, as long as this annoyance, this insect, is extracted from the suave ointment of empire.

Perhaps, who knows, the accused has objected publicly to the violence of the king, to his weaponry, his wars. Leave it at that. Wisdom sits in judgment. We shall shortly know her mind:

Now the Wisdom of God, Sophia, comes forth, reaching from "end to

end mightily." She wills also to be the unseen pivot of all nature, the center and significance of all the light that is in all and for all.

> That which is poorest and humblest, that which is most
> hidden in all things, is nevertheless most obvious in them,
> and quite manifest, for it is their own self that stands be-
> fore us, naked and without care.

("Hagia Sophia," Thomas Merton)

How could She not rule in favor of "that which is poorest and hum-
blest?"

✦ ✦ ✦

6:22 We shall make allowance for the vastly unpersuasive fiction of
our author. In the text, what chances she takes, what ventures!

The trope is sublimely daring. To wit: the Solomon of the historical
Bible is steeped in Wisdom. More, he conducts the holy One through the
centuries, in our direction. On the tides of the world and time she comes.

And for Her sake, for Her gifts, we give heed, putting aside for the nonce
our reservations.

We willingly enter a darkness of surmise. The court is like a cave of the
Ardennes: there anciently, "from the very beginning," Wisdom has left
traces of her presence, drawings irreplaceable, wondrous to behold.

For our sake, what message is written there, what images on the walls?
What mean the hieroglyphics?

✦ ✦ ✦

An introduction. And we pause.

Do the words sit ill on the tongue of such as Solomon? Do we hesitate
to enter the counsels of the profane? No matter, the words sit well on
another tongue, that of the author, who has shown ample proof of
Wisdom.

(And a thought. Can it be that he places wise words in the mouth of
folly, only as a covert instruction, a "beware"? Or at least a "go slow"—
since even the foolish occasionally may flash out a beam of wisdom?)

✦ ✦ ✦

6:23–25 A further caveat: the author will not allow a "consuming jeal-
ousy" to invade his words . . .

The declaration is local to his circumstance, and surely relevant elsewhere—and elsewhen. He is not flogging a mystery religion, nor excreting
the liverish bile of academe. Neither of which, he notes handily, has "anything in common with true Wisdom."

Amen to that. Let us hear loud and clear the apothegm, untrammeled, rare, from the mouth of Wisdom herself:

> A multitude
> of the wise
>
> is the salvation
> of the world (6:24)

We take it to heart. And we mourn. "A multitude"? How sparse the virtue, how few to claim it in truth!

And among world authorities? Not one.

✦ ✦ ✦

> Wisdom decrees:
> A wise ruler
> is the salvation
> of the people (6:24)

Wisdom so decrees. And we? Alas, behold our plight, citizens of the dark Realm of the Opposite. Certifiable fools and nebbishes hold authority in our nation. They declare themselves masters of the world economy. They misbehave on a vast scale, rattling nuclear sabers, bombing, sanctioning against the innocent, threatening the creation.

Still, we do not despair. Wisdom does not permit so easy a luxury.

If there is no "multitude of the wise"—and one doubts if such a fullness of the wise has ever visited our poor planet—still, there are a few. Seek them out then, heed their counsel.

And if in the ruler there is no wisdom? (If in Solomon himself, there is little or no wisdom?) Then at least (at most!), ensure that among the ruled, at least a few be wise.

✦ ✦ ✦

As for the ruler, the dictum holds: suffer a fool—and not necessarily gladly. There are other, better resources, other friends. Befriend them. And keep the mind's edge sharp, like an irritant in an oyster's guts.

chapter five

Solomon at prayer: "I sought Wisdom for counsel and comfort . . ." (7:1–9:18)

7:1–7 A remarkable, condensed "autobiography of deflation" follows. The sense: let us bring imperial greatness down to size, let humans concede their human limits.

In effect, this fictive, idealized Solomon is not inclined to play God: "I am only a mortal."

And we breathe easier, even as we recall the many occasions when he exceeded all moral boundaries.

No more of that. The selfless genius of our author! No point in opening old wounds, or flogging the dead. The text is forgiving, and offers a noble revision.

Let us than take advantage of an altered repute, deserved or no. Let us hearken to this purified Solomon, to the honor of Wisdom. For her sake, let us indulge in a noble fiction.

Let the author compose a drama, Greek at that. Let him place over his own features the golden mask of Solomon.

And lo! Majesty Reborn steps forth, announces himself, purveyor of Wisdom.

✦   ✦   ✦

The intent is clear. King Solomon, no hero to the peers or subjects of his lifetime, must be made useful to the needs of his descendants. Draw him forth then from the tomb, a new creation.

We recall the social scene: the Jews in diaspora, in danger of the sweet cheat, religious and cultural assimilation.

Who shall signal the danger, who offer another way? Legendary Solomon must be summoned, cleansed of the detritus and scandals of his last years. Let him be reborn, a vessel of Wisdom brimming as in the days of youth.

Summon him: the Solomon who was attentive to the grief of two nameless prostitutes. A *Magister* of Wisdom *non pareil*, who cut the Gordian knot

that bound the dead child and the living. Solomon the wise, who in rumor and awe, passed into immortality.

✦　✦　✦

This revised royal one is wonderfully chastened. It is as though in the centuries since his demise, he were detained in limbo or suspended in purgation. Then he returns to us, a Lazarus figure, chastened in ego, wide of eye, anxious in a childlike way to join himself, newly human, to our lot.

Come in, come in! We admit him gladly. Enough to know that he will respect the ethic and behavior binding on all: an ethic that binds with adamant—let it be said once more—the kings of earth.

He, a king who fell into idolatry, summons his peers: let them show forth their (so rare) best.

✦　✦　✦

On the lips of Wisdom, Solomon's instruction is majestic, astringent, befitting. One ventures that our author has studied great Aeschylus:

> No ruler
> has different origin
> or birth:

one
is the entry into life
for all,

in one
same way
they leave it (7:5–6)

Legend or fact, what matter? The author recalls the famous prayer of Solomon, seeking above all, Wisdom. The prayer is summoned repeatedly in the historic books (1 Kings 3:6–9; 5:9–14; and again, 2 Chronicles 1:8–10).

Historic, legendary, or mixed and mingling with both. The prayer, we are told, was granted. And more: because the king sought only Wisdom, all was granted beside. And the best of both worlds (or the best together with the worst!) descended.

✦ ✦ ✦

Alas, the young Regent of Wisdom became a notorious, conspicuous wastrel of gifts and grants. And a sea change followed. The double grant of wisdom and incomparable riches proved an unworkable duo.

Mortal life tore the gifts apart. But wonder of wonders, Solomon *redivivus* joins them in one: no danger attending, no shadow corrupting. Only a single intermingled blessing:

All good things

came together
with Wisdom,

and countless riches
at her hands (5:11)

The latter part of the story, the decline and fall, is ignored as a mere excrescence. It is beside his point—the point of this Solomon twice born.

✦ ✦ ✦

7:8–14 Now let the king, purified and single of mind, praise his treasure, Wisdom.

In our lifetime Thomas Merton, himself twice born, grasped the spirit of the paean. And no wonder: the monk too underwent a rite of passage, a transformation. Surely he writes of himself:

In Wisdom there are no reasons and no answers. Yet she is the candor of God's light, the expression of God's simplicity. . . .

All that is sweet in her tenderness will speak on all sides in everything, without ceasing . . .

(One so endowed) will never be the same again.

He will awaken not to conquest and dark pleasure but to
the impeccable pure simplicity of One consciousness in all
and through all: one Wisdom, one Child, one Meaning,
one Sister.

("Hagia Sophia," Thomas Merton)

✦   ✦   ✦

No assimilation to the Greeks in our text of Wisdom, but a wondrous
form of "reverse enculturation." An instance also of deft literary genius:
into the hands of Solomon, our author places the exorbitant scope of Greek
culture.

And we note the daring "more": by implication he declares, "we are
the ones!" Surely a social and cultural transfer of considerable daring: he
attributes the greatness of the Greeks, in philosophy, science, drama—to
his own people, the Hebrew minority.

✦   ✦   ✦

Many are the implications here, in honor of both Jew and Greek.

We witness a sublime spiritual larceny in which neither side is dimin-
ished. Subtly, a claim is made of a fine Jewish flowering. And concurrently
a tribute is laid at the feet of indigenous genius, of the tragedians, Plato
and Aristotle, the Stoics.

With this subtle, crucial addition—or subtraction. In knowledge of God,
in faith in God, we Jews owe nothing to Greeks.

The point is made, one thinks, with considerable courage. The Hebrew-
Greek experiment has issued in a seamless graft and a mutual
flowering—Wisdom conferred on both Greek and Jew. But with a difference: only the Hebrews can preface the achievement with a sublime act of
fealty, of needful submission, of faith. Only they can declare: We believe.

Be it underscored as well: the prayer of Solomon is here greatly
enlarged from the original. In order, one thinks, to make the original point,
in a far different circumstance, unmistakably lucid.

Let the Greeks know it: Solomon's wisdom was no merely human
attainment. It was a borrowing of the divine Fullness, here acknowledged
as such:

> God grant me
> suitable speech,
>
> valuing
> these endowments
> at their true worth.

For God
is the sure guide
of Wisdom,

and the director
of the wise.

We
and our words
are in God's hand,

we
and our discourse,
intelligence,
skills.

It is God
who grants me

sound knowledge
of existing things . . . (7:15–17)

✦   ✦   ✦

7:22–25 And it is as though a dazzling flowering carpet unrolled, beneath the feet of royal Wisdom. See it and wonder—twenty one species of blossoms, the total of absolute perfection!

The nuanced tribute of communality continues. Jewish hands and Greek have labored together to weave the carpet. (Among both, a mystique of numbers flourishes, as our author is careful to note).

But communality goes only so far. The carpet is edged with a strict border: none may tread beyond. Jewish monotheism must, and does, remain intact.

And again, let Plato and the philosophers celebrate the bouquet of attributes, the glories of Wisdom, handing them over to the "world soul, the *Nous*, the *Logos*."

Not our author. Supple there, firm here, an ecumenical soul stops short of syncretism. So he stands near the border of the carpet, making a simple, needful point. He stands and points to—the Beyond. All glory to Wisdom, the sublime attribute of—God.

✦   ✦   ✦

Wisdom celebrated! We are invited to ponder, perhaps even to recite aloud the litany of praise. In so doing we are praising God.

Could it be put more firmly, the living connection, the feminine aura of the Holy?

> She
> is breath
> of the might of God,
>
> pure effusion
> of the glory
> of the all Powerful (7:25).

And the image of Light:

> She,
> refulgence
> of eternal light,
>
> spotless mirror
> of the power of God,
>
> image of God's goodness (7:26)

✦   ✦   ✦

7:26 The image is endlessly suggestive, like light begetting light, mirror flashing off mirror.

This light is more excellent than every created light,

> . . . is fairer
> than the sun,
>
> surpasses
> every constellation.
>
> Compared to light
> she
> takes precedence,
>
> for day
> must yield
> to night:
>
> but wickedness
> over Wisdom
>
> prevails never (7:29–30)

✦   ✦   ✦

The rabbis for their part, were endlessly enchanted with the implications of God and light, God as Light:

Since the sun was not created until the fourth day, whence did light have its origin?

Two answers were given to the question. One rabbi affirmed: "the holy One, blessed be He, enwrapped Himself in light like a garment, and the brilliance of His splendor shone forth from one end of the universe to the other."

The second rabbi maintained that light emanated from the site of the temple, which . . . was the center of the earth's creation . . .

Both utterances express the same thought: i.e., only through the medium of the spiritual light which radiates from God, could chaos be reduced to order (Talmud).

✦   ✦   ✦

Our Christian testament will make much ado, and many a midrash of the same image:

> This Son
> is reflection
> of the Father's glory,
>
> exact likeness
> of God's own being (Hebrews 1:3)

✦   ✦   ✦

> Christ is image
> of the invisible God . . . (Colossians 1:15)

✦   ✦   ✦

> The real Light
>
> —which gives light
> to every human—
>
> was coming
> into the world (John 1:9)

✦   ✦   ✦

Thus too the mystics:

> When the recluses of fourteenth-century England heard their church bells and looked out upon the worlds and fens under a kind sky, they spoke in their hearts to "Jesus our Mother."
>
> It was Sophia who had awakened in their childlike hearts.
>
> ("Hagia Sophia," Thomas Merton)

✦ ✦ ✦

Vision

Then showed me God
in right hand held everything that is

The hand was a woman's,
creation all lusty
a meek bird's egg

resting there waiting
her Word and I heard it:

"newborn I make you
nestling I love you
homing I keep you"

DB

✦ ✦ ✦

7:27 She is godly, this Wisdom. More, She is God. Apprehensible, omnipotent, God performing the works of God in the world. And behold Her supreme work, God creating the godly amid ourselves:

> She,
> being One,
> can do all things.
>
> Unchanging,
> she renews all.
>
> From age to age,
> She is poured
> into holy souls:
>
> She creates
> friends of God
> and prophets (7:27)

✦ ✦ ✦

Indeed She creates "friends of God." In our gospel the glance of Jesus falls on His own: and the phrase leaps to his tongue:

> "You are My friends
>
> if you do
> what I command you . . .
>
> I call you friends.
>
> I have made known to you

all
that I heard
from My Father" (John 15: 14–15)

And a Greek inference as well: among the philosophers, a sage was known as "friend of the god."

✦   ✦   ✦

7:28 The imagery grows daring, we are drawn into the nuptial chamber of the Song of Songs, of Hosea, Ezekiel, Isaiah:

There is no one
beloved of God

except the spouse
Wisdom (7:28)

✦   ✦   ✦

8:1–9 Solomon intrudes, for the moment, lightly.

Remarkable once more is the imprint of Greek mind upon the page. Plato's *Phaedra* walks there, "lover of Wisdom's beauty." And the mystery religions as well: "Wisdom, instructor in knowledge of God."

And the Stoics, their "four virtues" incorporated in the Christian "cardinal virtues" of temperance, prudence, justice, and courage.

The scope of Wisdom is nothing short of prodigious. And the authorial genius as well, what depth and range!

In this scribe, Wisdom has met her match, and happily. A coruscating magician of image and word, he borrows, embraces, transforms. It is as though he held in two arms the grand bouquet of creation, and scattered flowers along the path of time, for us to follow, and gather. And who knows, even grow wise.

In prose constantly verging on poetry, ardent and urbane he proffers Wisdom in all her glory.

Shall we name him a genius? The word, one thinks, falls short. The Greeks among whom he moves so easily, Plato, Socrates, Aeschylus, the Stoics, the votaries of Mysteries—these are geniuses.

He is a friend of these towering spirits. But one senses that his deep soul belongs in other company, finally. He has been formed by the Wisdom he celebrates: he is among the "friends of God and the prophets."

And how blessed we are! Through him, the Incomprehensible nears.

✦ ✦ ✦

In accord with the literary fiction, our author has had his say.

Now great Solomon emerges and raises his voice.

And at this point a subtle change of tone emerges. It is as though a sublime, faultless dawn were shortly overtaken by a wrack of clouds, and a storm.

The high mood falters, the supreme fiction loses its center.

We have raised the question before: perhaps ever so indirectly, doubt is overtaking our serendipitous author.

The doubt: can such as Solomon be rehabilitated?

✦ ✦ ✦

We hear the blare of trumpets—or perhaps of royal ego.

A seeming embodiment of nobility strides on stage. And true nobility lags behind like a miming court fool. We are offered a new protagonist. *Eccolo*, great Solomon *redivivus*! His bearing, his male aura is self-approving, assured, beyond critique, a regent in the instructional mode.

✦ ✦ ✦

Let us suggest a deconstruction of the author's intent.

Is the altered climate deliberate? Does our friend of Wisdom remain master of the text, injecting here a subtle dose of irony? Is Solomon, heady with purported wisdom, being ever so deftly put down?

In any case, a lesson strikes, hard. With the royal entrance we have lost greatly: substance and momentum, an airy spirit, the Pivot of all, gift and its Giver, the Hand gently cherishing creation and tendering it into our hands. All this, lost. For a time.

✦ ✦ ✦

We come to earth with a thump. Solomon lays claim to Wisdom. But, but. How lamentably he falls short of Her poverty, Her self-emptying mercy.

Solomon's wisdom? Let us modify the term, the reality. He is clever and adroit, apt in the circumlocutions maneuverings of the kings of earth.

He claims Wisdom for his own: we are inclined to doubt that he can bring the claim off.

Sword, scepter, orb, crown, those mighty impediments against Her modesty and mercy.

✦　✦　✦

Wisdom can be written or spoken about, only as "The Other," the "she." The rule is well understood by our author. Thus the Mystery stands at a distance, inviolate.

Kings are another matter, impatient as they are with realities that elude their basilisk eye. They all but demand that Sophia be summoned to stand before them. She is, so to speak, their due, another subject, a prerequisite of their rank.

Who knows? She might prove useful.

✦　✦　✦

The tone changes, abruptly—it darkens. We shift to the first person: King Solomon is pleased to launch on his autobiography.

And the "I" par excellence is loud on the air. In principle, the royal ego is impatient of "The Other," the "she."

Now supposing that this "she" is a Person, is The Person, is the ineffable Hagia Sophia, we hear a lofty resolve wafting like a ribbon of smoke from the solomonic tongue:

"I determined to take her to live with me."

May there not be implied an ambiguity as to the author's intent?

Ambiguity and an implied instruction, with ourselves in mind?

It is as though in the eye of the king, Wisdom were featureless, of no greater moment than a member of the king's harem.

✦　✦　✦

Let us push matters. Might ambiguity be the author's intent? Might he wish that we decide for ourselves this strange matter of King Solomon and his "wisdom," referred to as another possession, perhaps a preferred concubine? Might the author even invite us to generalize?

He presents great Solomon as bumptious, a bit foolish. Are we to grow skeptical then, as to the claim that Wisdom dwells in possession (sic) of kings?

✦　✦　✦

Sophia dwells where Sophia chooses to dwell. Our skepticism, inherited from so noble a source, might indicate that Hagia Sophia freely, and with a kind of delicious irony, resides elsewhere than among the fabled great ones. Might she prefer the lowly habitation of our own hearts?

Speculation, to be sure, but of the sort beloved of rabbis. And perhaps not entirely bootless.

✦ ✦ ✦

Such was the royal design: Hagia Sophia was appointed the king's counselor and consolation. In good times and bad, she would stand by him.

He began his reign auspiciously, at age fourteen, as the historian
Josephus tells us. The royal arrangement prospered for awhile.

Eventually, veritable hammer blows fell, such contingencies as are raised
and lowered by the arm of fate. Such batterings as are unforeseen, even
unavoidable, by the Solomons of this world.

Sophia departed the court, whether in sorrow or relief, we are not told.
And the king? In years to come, and in mockery of hoary locks and a
purportedly wise old age, his behavior would do no honor to a court fool.

✦ ✦ ✦

During those awful years Hagia Sophia could not pluck the king from
excesses and follies. Which perhaps is a hint, and more: that his brand of
"wisdom" remained foreign, even repugnant to Her dignity—to Herself.

Foreign, perhaps odious. To this outcome: Her departure spelled disaster for the king. It was as though She, forgetful of native mildness, turned
like a Fury on him and his counterfeit wisdom.

✦ ✦ ✦

8:10–16 A simulacrum of wisdom? Words lumber on, the tone of the
king's autobiography grows wearying, self-congratulatory.

And we speculate. Is there humor in the air, glee within earshot, as the
stroking and puffing goes on? No dismissing the possibility: our author is
a master of subtlety.

(The savants of BJ miss the humor entirely. Commenting on 8:16, they
inform us loftily that Solomon did not live up to his noble ideal. But it is
hardly the intent of the author to dwell upon the weaknesses of the Royal-
Sage (sic).

The author of Chronicles had already paid the great king (sic) a like
homage of silence.

(One all but sees the author smiling at the starchy apodictics. Only set
the ego of the Royal-Sage loose on the page: he will put to naught the
"homage of silence.")

✦ ✦ ✦

The monologue has the leaden tone of an edict or an encyclical. To all
intent, we are to take his word for his word concerning himself.

Urbi et orbi, this. It is the royal pleasure that everyone, youth and sage,
friend and enemy, consort and concubine, subject and vanquished, the

dead and the favored generations to come—that all pay tribute and bow low. Solomon is simply the greatest, the most virtuous, vigilant, valiant, avuncular king to be discovered anywhere on the earth's round:

> . . . and in war
> courageous.
>
> I return
> to my dwelling,
>
> taking repose
> beside her . . . (8:15–16)

The durable fiction, the impermeable self-congratulation!

✦   ✦   ✦

8:17–21 We are invited back in time, to Solomon's childhood. Wisdom, true or false, has not yet been conferred, nor is need of the gift apprehended.

Then the need dawns, the lack is felt, as the young prince comes to maturity.

How then shall he take wisdom for his own? By way, we are told, of piety. He must pray to God for the gift of God. Sound.

But still, ambiguous. The intent of the author remains cloudy. Is the young king on the right way, or the errant? Is his god, the god of an overweening temple and its vast bureaucracy, including a squad of priest-functionaries—is this god to be equated with Hagia Sophia?

Is the god of Solomon's wars and wealth apt to give into the king's hands this meek innocent One, the merciful, the tender, the plenary in grace?

✦   ✦   ✦

Is Solomon's god our God?

We pause over a momentous question. Our knowledge of the Holy, of Hagia Sophia, of God in Jesus—this hovers above the narrative. One almost thinks: this is at stake here.

✦   ✦   ✦

We have suggested before that the author of Wisdom, that *magister* of hint and nuance, chooses to ignore the follies of the king. For the chronicler's own reasons, to be sure.

On this hypothesis, our author sets Solomon free to inhabit the page as chief actor of the drama. Alone, uninhibited, creating his image—with, so to speak, no outsider's slant, no third party interjection.

With what intent? Perhaps to catch the conscience of the king, to allow

Solomon to reveal Solomon. All unwitting, the royal discourse, its windy rhetoric, will reveal the king's vanity and self-deception.

And what of the quality and source of his famed "wisdom"? Was the Spirit of God, Hagia Sophia, truly bestowed on the king? Let believers read and ponder. They will come to know much of Solomon.

Much too of the quality of their own faith.

✦ ✦ ✦

9:1–18 The prayer acknowledges many borrowings. It draws upon another account of the same invocation (1 Kings 3:6–9). Lengthier than the original, this version is in debt to other wisdom sources, and adds elements reflective of the author's own faith. The prayer is majestic, polished to perfection: the royal sentiments are beyond reproach.

They are also somewhat tedious.

✦ ✦ ✦

9:3–4 Can a king be other than two-faced? According to Solomon, kings such as he were created

> to govern the creation
> with sanctity and justice,
>
> to rule the empire
> with an upright spirit (9:3)

One face of Solomon, one thinks, is turned to God in prayer. The king repeats faultlessly the catechesis of the book of Beginnings.

The implication? Home truths of creation converge, are brought to bear on—himself. He, the triumph of the creation.

Then, another, far different face. Solomon is after all, a king, which is to say, a pragmatist, a creator of things, bigger, better, richer, more stupendous. He is—(and how is one to do justice to this seismic accommodation?)—the ineffable, the invincible, the audacious, the front-runner in the race toward world eminence.

Power generates the will and appetite for—more power. Then let power accumulate in the royal person and projects: power must overpower—whether citizens, rivals, enemies.

So. Solomon creates a system of forced labor and a standing army, undertakes incursive wars, accumulates vast riches, raises a stupendous temple and palace.

His inner circle prospers, riches fatten the prospering few. And multitudes languish in poverty.

Whether all this transpires with the connivance of his god is left moot. Left perhaps to ourselves.

It seems that in spite of the above divagations, the frown of the god casts no shadow over our pages.

✦   ✦   ✦

As to the king's prayer, one would hesitate to term it a conscious lie. Self-deceived, let us say: he contrives a verbal spin. Solomon has lost the common touch: language follows suit.

To illustrate. Here, a system of injustice can be presented straight-faced to God, as good and sound, its sponsor meritorious, its substance without stain.

In his own eyes and those of his acolytes, the king is an icon of everything *dignum et justum* under the sun. Should not the praise of the god then follow suit? Or better, should the deity not lead the accolade?

Is the god deceived by the prayer, or is the god perhaps complicit in the imperial dream and deed? It is left to us.

One matter would seem clear. In light (or darkness) of an onerous system, phrases like "holiness and justice," "integrity of spirit"—these sound hollow as a war drum.

✦   ✦   ✦

9:5–12 The king, it would seem, is led to characterize himself before God. It appears that the god requires this: or perhaps the king's ego. In any case, he proceeds to the task, with an eager, even groveling gusto.

Talk about glorying in infirmities! Solomon is

> the son
> of your handmaid,
> a weak man,
> as to allotted years—
> ephemeral.
>
> Slow
> in comprehension
> of justice and law (9:5)

✦   ✦   ✦

"Son of your handmaid," i.e., "of your slave," is instructive. The fiction: Solomon is a slave, born in slavery rather than purchased. Thus his bond with the slave owner (sic) stands the more firm.

One wonders. Does he protest too much, does he bow so low as to lose balance?

Is he presented here as sincere—or as otherwise, a poseur? Our wise author leaves space within the text, inviting us to ponder.

✦ ✦ ✦

Ponder we do. As to ourselves, what image do we present to the Deity—we as slaves, friends, brothers, lovers? And what of that allegation: the two faces of Solomon, the fulsome, majestic prayer—and in his empire, the shameful injustice that festered away?

What human system does his god approve, what abominate?

And what of our God?

✦ ✦ ✦

In a sense, and much to the mind of Solomon, the god is in debt to the king. To put the matter bluntly (and of course the matter is never so stated), his highness is simply owed this boon of Wisdom.

So let the matter be merely touched, as fingers touch in a minuet.

Let the king recall the close connections forged in his youth between the almighty and himself. He was chosen over his brothers to rule Israel. Under divine mandate he undertook the construction of the grand temple. And the god was pleased to dwell there.

Therefore, shall it not be implied ever so delicately—that a debt comes due?

The logic of memory: O canny king, so persuasive, so possessive!

✦ ✦ ✦

No denying it, the prayer is nobly spoken. By implication, the king's record is here cleansed of default, of bloodletting wars and domestic injustice. We marvel at the skill of our author, contriving this royal persona, twice born.

A hope, a strange one dawns in the mind: even kings may be cleansed. And a further grace. A royal rogue, it would seem, may compose a worthy prayer. Let him then do so, for our sake as well.

And what lofty sentiments he would have us raise, before God and before Sophia, the mighty and meek!

> that She
> may be with me
> and labor with me,
>
> that I
> may know
> Your good pleasure (9:10)

Indeed, pray on! Sophia holds high office and renders crucial service to mortals, be these great Solomon or ourselves. The king speaks for all:

She
will guide me
discreetly
in my affairs

and safeguard me by Her glory (9:11)

A puzzling phrase, at first blush: Sophia protecting the king through "Her glory." Until perhaps, we recall the overshadowing "shekinah" of the desert years, the "cloud by day" and "pillar of fire by night" guiding the nomad tribe.

✦   ✦   ✦

Thus
my deeds

will be acceptable
to You,

I
shall govern Your people
with justice,

becoming worthy
of my father's throne (9:12)

No caviling with the rightness of the petition, together with its implied invitation—to recall the munificent prospering, as well as its sorry outcome.

We recall the sequence. His reign knew a sound beginning. So noble a prayer merited the presence of Sophia: for awhile. Then, mortally offended, she withdrew.

And shortly, Her absence opened a void and hell descended to earth. Injustice and war proliferated, the realm fell apart like a rotting corpse. One after another a series of corrupt killers, inventive in evil, morally dwarfish, mounted the throne, fell and were replaced by worse.

✦   ✦   ✦

9:13–15 The mortal lot: the unknown, the future, that enigma.

Beyond doubt, to penetrate it (more frequently, to live with it!) is the gift of Sophia—a sense of limits. A sense of mortality as well, knowing nothing of the outcome of our lives, whether meritorious or lamentable. Possibly, awfully, an outcome lamentable as that of great Solomon.

Sophia sets us trembling in our bones. trembling for the king and his like, as they topple in ruin. And for ourselves, walking as we must amid the Cloud of Unknowing.

✦ ✦ ✦

Meaning within meaning. Are the verses offered as examples of Wisdom conferred on the King, mournfully (and unwontedly!) confessing to the human lot—he also steeped in ignorance, in the frailty endemic to our lot? Certainly, these are so offered.

Are the verses to be thought as well, examples of Wisdom conferred on the author himself? Just as certainly, one thinks.

And are the same verses offered as an instruction to the unborn, to ourselves? Offered as a corrective of cultural myths of omniscience and omnipotence? Equally.

✦ ✦ ✦

Once more manifest is our author's spirit of generous ecumenism. Verses 14–16 envision an "anthropology of limits" reminiscent of Plato and Sophocles:

> The deliberations
> of mortals
>
> how timid,
> how unsure our designs.
>
> For
> the corruptible body
> burdens the soul,
> and an earthen shelter
> weighs down the mind
> with a thousand cares.

A like version of the human is offered by Paul:

> This treasure (i.e., the glory of God, shining in the face of Christ) we possess in earthly vessels, to make clear that its surpassing power comes from God and not from ourselves (2 Corinthians 4:7)

✦ ✦ ✦

9:16–18 Great Solomon in the days of his glory

> . . . surpassed in riches and wisdom all the kings of earth.

> And the whole world sought audience with Solomon, to hear from him the wisdom which God had put in his heart (1 Kings 10:23)

Here, in sharp contrast, perhaps in correction, the king confesses to a human scope. Gracefully, but unmistakably.

In the extravagant original account, no such humbling word intruded. Another instance of authorial genius. It is as though the ghost of Solomon were to reappear, a revenant from purgatory, chastened in sackcloth and ashes. Toppled from pride of place, he bespeaks a new wisdom, wrung from sorrow and loss:

> Scarce
> do we guess
> the things of earth:
>
> what is well within grasp
> we understand
> with difficulty.
>
> When matters
> are of heaven,
> how
> search them out? (9:16)

To raise the question is to raise the ante. Urgently we pray: Come, holy Spirit!

And the response? With Sophia, abundant and without blame, to ask is to receive, to seek is to find. The king cries aloud with longing, Come! And sweetly attentive she responds:

> Who
> came on Your counsel,
>
> except
> You had given Sophia
>
> and sent
>
> Your holy Spirit
> from on high? (9:17)

✦   ✦   ✦

We learn from God's word the depth of our plight, our Fall, a free fall while time lasts. Bottomless the pit into which, but for her . . .

Thanks to Her, our Fall is penultimate, not our fate, not final.

To break the Fall, Someone has placed himself in mortal jeopardy. We have fallen not into hell: literally, we have fallen on—Another.

These verses announce a merciful intervention. *Redivivus*, Solomon comes, his soul alight with Wisdom, to instruct us.

He is like the ghost of Hamlet's father, telling from a chastened mouth, truths hidden from the earthbound:

> Your will,
> who
> could know it . . . ?

The question hangs on the air. Without that Intervention, pure and unmerited, we are lost. Fallen. Knowing little or nothing of our place in the scheme of creation, nothing of boundaries, of the true way.

✦ ✦ ✦

Hagia Sophia is at our service: to entreat Her is to receive. And receiving, one confesses, even rejoices in, Her Presence.

She is daring, without fear. She has come—to dwell even with a soul from purgatory.

She would storm the gates of hell, if entreated. Look. She enters hell on earth, and transforms all—

> Thus were the paths
> of the earthbound
> made straight,
>
> and humans learned
> what gave You
> good pleasure,
>
> and
> by Hagia Sophia
> they were saved (9:18)

✦ ✦ ✦

If the likes of Solomon were saved, if Sophia plucked him, a brand from the burning, is there not hope for all?

We take the oracle seriously. It sings of hope amid hell on earth.

The trodden paths are crooked and cruel and lead nowhere. That is the sum of it, of our century, of the millennium past.

And if the past were our only prospect, what of the doomed, awful millennia to come?

But for Sophia's intervention, sweet and strong, we humans are bound nowhere, and fast—our passage in the world a blur of incoherence, a self-destroying spasm. A millennium has closed. In its course we have repeated, crime for crime, the sins of Solomon, dramatizing anew the decline and fall of the solomonic empire. In ferocious ambition, what crimes we have committed in the world!

The "century of America" has spiraled down and down: war, greed in the ascendancy, contempt for the "widow and orphan," militarized diplomacy, sanctions and air strikes, domestic misery.

Across the world, Sophia weeps amid the ruins. To this her vocation is reduced: She weeps amid the ruins, the rubble of her hope. And did we but know it, the rubble of our own.

Has hope come to this: weeping amid the rubble of hope?

Do not despise tears, or grief where grieving is due. Dwell there, be mindful. Her hope and ours, if we but knew it, are one and the same. God's hope and ours.

chapter six

"Wisdom delivers the just from among the wicked . . ." (10:1–21)

10:1–14 Sophia in history, our God immersed in time, mourning for our sin. Sophia, Witness from the beginning.

And how strange: in this story of holy Accompaniment, no human is named. Anonymity is the order of day. And this holds firm, though each of the great ones, including notorious sinners, is manifestly (one thinks even stubbornly), accompanied.

Sophia clings to the human venture, shadows us, birth to death. Welcomed as Sister, Lover, Friend, Counselor—or unwanted, despised, shunted aside. Received and welcomed, or shunted aside, this Angel Guardian of saints and sinners.

Amid the turmoil of history, She walks with us. Close as a shadow all of light, or far distant, unwanted: still She walks with us. No one abandoned, no one unprotected, despised, expendable.

Sophia perseveres, this Pilgrim Sister. See Her at our side! From "the first formed father of the world," to "the sinner," to "the just one," to another "just one" and "his child," to yet another "just one," to a "pillar of salt." On and on she trudges, beside a fourth "just one," who receives much attention, and "his brother," who merits little.

And yet another, this one well known to us: a "just man, sold."

✦　✦　✦

It is as though the protagonists of our history appeared and vanished: their guise is masked or veiled.

The literary device of absolute anonymity is puzzling, invites pondering. Perhaps the author would place sin and blame at a safe remove, that individuals might be seen as instructive types of the human—or the inhuman?

And again, why name names, when Everyman/woman must by implication trudge the same ground?

More, the iteration of "just" gives hope: in the eyes of Wisdom, the just by far outnumber the wicked.

Again. The anonymity mitigates, softens crime, without in any way denying its perduring strain, even as the device places in strong relief the sanctifying unction of the presence of Sophia. It is She who anoints Her own and pronounces them just, She, the Balm in Gilead.

✦   ✦   ✦

10:15–17 The scene widens, vastly. Yet the new phase is social and personal, both. Now Sophia accompanies

> the holy people,
> the blameless race . . .
>
> as they depart from slavery in Egypt (10:15)

The phrase is unprecedented, paying tribute to a singular greatness. Sophia

> enters the soul
> of one
> faithful to God (10:16)

That soul will be held firm by Sophia: and necessarily so! How else except through her, shall Moses, savior, lawgiver, mystic, and prophet be protected, and prevail?

✦   ✦   ✦

Her succoring the people in flight recalls an image dear to the author of Exodus: "a Shekinah by day, a pillar of fire by night."

Here too, the miraculous is gently incorporated, folded in natural phenomena: Sophia serves as

> a shelter
> by day,
>
> and fiery stars
> by night (10:17)

✦   ✦   ✦

10:18–20 The tone alters. A memory both vindictive and ecstatic is aroused. (Does the contrast dwell in the mind of Sophia, or perhaps in the author of our book?)

The vengeance of the wronged dies hard, how hard!

All unexpected, a bolt of lightning from a clear sky, much is made of victory and the swamping of enemies. Horrid details are multiplied and magnified: they surpass by far the episodes of Exodus.

We are told, for example, that corpses of the enemy were stripped of their arms, a ghoulish detail untold elsewhere.

A regression?

We had not thought it befitting to our beloved Sophia, or ethically plausible: the canticle of Moses is rehearsed in its main theme.

The god has granted victory to his (sic) own:

> The Lord
> is a warrior . . .
>
> Pharaoh's chariots and armor
> he has cast
> into the sea . . .
>
> Your right hand,
> O god
>
> has shattered the enemy . . .
>
> And more of the like.

✦ ✦ ✦

10:21 Then our author offers a curious conclusion. The victory was granted

Because Wisdom

> opened
> the mouths of the dumb
>
> and to infants
> gave ready speech (10:21)

Hyperbole? Strangely apt in any case, if one thinks of mute slaves, recently freed.

chapter seven

Exodus, and "You love all, and loath nothing of what You have made" (11:1–12:27)

11:1–5 Sophia simply disappears from the text.

Perhaps her work, as such, is done. Her complex historical vocation has been revealed: the outpouring of God's Goodness in Her accompaniment of us humans—and this in face of the crime and evil that pursue the Fallen like a plague. She, Healer of the plague, if only the plague-ridden consent to Her healing.

Henceforth in our text another Name emerges: God, under a variety of images. God's breath (11:20), God's spirit (12:1), God's word (frequently: 12:9; 16:12; 18:15), God's hand (also frequently: 11:17; 14:6; 16:15; 19:8).

✦ ✦ ✦

We sense that under the quill of the master, we are losing nothing. The new litany of images is no less rich than those which graced Sophia—Who, all said, has revealed God in Her own guise.

Hagia Sophia, She for our delight.

And now God, shall we say, for our instruction.

In world and time, that Guardian Angel danced before us.

God will set a more sober pace, and summon a longer memory.

✦ ✦ ✦

11:6–14 The scene of Exodus will be recalled. The people have ventured into the desert, as far as the rock of Horeb. And a "murmuring," angry and waspish, rises against Moses.

"We die of thirst: why did you lead us out of Egypt?"

For their relief he struck the rock, and waters flowed free. That is the whole of it, according to Exodus (17: 1–7).

Numbers (20:2–13) however, tells the same story with an ominous slant. At Meribah, Moses struck the rock—twice.

Did he strike once in doubt, and a second time for reassurance? In any case, God was furious, the consequence dire: Moses and Aaron are forbidden to enter the Promise.

✦ ✦ ✦

And now another occasion, another audience. And a momentous question. Shall the author allow his people, in diaspora among the Greeks, to be shamed anew?

He shall not. He will keep his account, careful, consonant with the virtuous behavior of an "irreproachable tribe":

"In their thirst, the people [and we note: not Aaron and Moses] invoked You."

In the earlier account, they did not invoke God: to the contrary, they "murmured." They were, in the word of Moses, "rebels": there at Meribah they dared "put God to the test."

"And water was given them from the sheer rock."

✦ ✦ ✦

So begins a series of God's providential acts during the Exodus in the desert.

Seven antitheses are explored: in each, God unflinchingly favors his own, even as the Egyptians are heavily chastised.

Circumstance, it would seem, requires a new look at an old tale. One eye of our author rests on the author's tribe, another on the Alexandrian gentiles, beyond doubt closely observing.

✦ ✦ ✦

And the necessary question: with what tone, slant, nuance shall we Jews recall (and recount!) that tale—that favoring God, and our response?

Let us show in vivid detail, in vigorous, exemplary act, that "hand of God," that "arm of God"—protecting, cherishing his own—and at the same time, chastising our oppressors.

A different hint, another slant than the original is called for.

How vastly these Greeks differ from the enslaving Egyptians! And for that, what thanks are due our present hosts, what honor to be paid! In the new recounting therefore, let us underscore an abiding (and eminently useful) conviction. This: dispersed as we are, the favor of God abides. Our fidelity to God must be equally firm.

So we reserve to ourselves this favor: attendance at one philosophic school or another, picking and choosing, welcoming and rejecting. Whatever in this alluring culture serves to nourish our faith we adopt with thanks, and make our own. Whatever overtly or subtly contradicts our faith, we set aside.

✦   ✦   ✦

Beyond doubt we Jews rejoice in our favored circumstance. We revel in the wisdom of Heraclitus, Anaxagoras, Plato. We are willing debtors of Greek ideas and ideals: we welcome the honor paid to conscience, in those cardinal virtues adumbrated by the Greeks.

To the searching mind, your philosophers are endlessly attractive. From your great ones we draw precious nuances regarding Wisdom: initiation of humans into Her secrets, the omniscience and omnipresence of Spirit, the famed twenty-one attributes of Sophia. And so on.

✦   ✦   ✦

Thus too, history is brought to bear, our history, to be recounted amid Greeks as well. For sake of all, them and ourselves, the past is made available, the saving acts of God: that the present be rendered enlightened and holy.

We Jews would have the gentiles know it: through you, a favoring God continues to favor us. This is the encomium we offer our hosts: Greek genius is God's undiscriminating blessing.

Nor do we hesitate to reverse the matter, to dare this question: Great ones, what make you of this: we Jews are a form of God's favor toward you?

✦   ✦   ✦

God's favor, God's disfavor. Our ancestors were newly snatched from slavery: and the unconscionable slave masters and oppressors dogged them with might and main.

A story of water will highlight the contrast. For sake of the ex-slaves, miraculous waters were struck from rock.

And water was withheld from a people undeserving, who dared enslave others.

In the wilderness our people cried out to God, and the waters flowed. And the Egyptians? Their only source, the Nile, was turned to blood.

✦   ✦   ✦

We note the chiaroscuro, the master stroke of the artist, highlighting one detail, darkening another.

Did not the chosen murmur against God, sinning at the waters of Meribah, as Exodus reports? Wisdom chooses to purify the source, to cleanse the memory.

Sin? Nothing of the sort: only a cry of distress, followed by abundant response.

Contrast, highlight and shadow. Let the thirst of the faithful underscore the plight of the Egyptians:

> Showing the Hebrews
> through their thirst,
>
> with what (far worse) chastisement
> you struck their enemies (11:8)

The suffering of the Hebrews is medicinal, a "merciful correction." But
with the adversary, the intent darkens:

> The wicked,
> condemned in anger,
> were tormented. . . .
>
> As a stern king,
>
> you probed
> and condemned them (11:9–10)

Once again the skill. Alter the tone, suppress such facts as changed
circumstance renders redundant—or downright odious. Or at the least, of
no use to present intent.

Thus new circumstance demands a new way of recounting the story. It
is as though this were implied, this daring purpose: for all their genius,
these Greeks are deprived of the Gift given us. We Jews then, must offer
them homilies, occasions of faith.

How skilled is our author in the intellectual to-and-fro of the rabbis!

He also has an eye attentive to the main chance: how shall we Jews
flourish amid these extraordinary people?

Let ironies abound: let God's word alter God's word.

Hagia Sophia has not, after all, departed the world. Here, She sponsors
the method, with a vengeance: exegesis by way of midrash.

✦　✦　✦

Another point of a tale twice or thrice told. Historical memory has
softened and hardened, both.

Of what moment, in view of the triumphant outcome of Exodus (all
praise to the regal line, to Saul and David and great Solomon!)—of what
moment that small mishap at Meribah? It falls in place: a mere gaffe
along the way.

Granted, our people failed the test, perhaps even great Moses failed.
The memory is dim, and moot. But surely minor. Did not the rewarding
water flow free?

And was not a like benefit denied the oppressors? It was.

Their thirst unquenched was the punishment:

> their perennial river
>
> was troubled
> with impure blood (11:6)

◆ ◆ ◆

The offense, the enslavement, the generational humiliation, brick-making without straw, the lethal decree against our firstborn . . . These, and many another crimes against our ancestors lie in memory, hardened to a cobalt.

You Greeks, glorying in citizenship and freedom, must understand: slavery was sin, institutionalized, mortised into a "second nature." What befell us would befall, immemorially: there were to be slaves and slave masters. We were to abandon hope. We were in hell.

An image: imperial Egypt took the form of a great pyramid. The pharaoh, standing at summit, bore down and down. And we were condemned to the base, crushed there to a rubble.

◆ ◆ ◆

Thus the tribal memory. It is highly selective, and builds its case, unassailably. This: the innocence of the offended—who are also, and ineluctably, the chosen.

Memory is retroactive as well: it creates new images to justify the offended, before God and history.

Here memory summons a "twofold grief": it rises like a miasma to torment the Egyptians (and of such an onset of remorse, we discover not a word in Exodus).

And that theme of water and no water: how it persists! Chagrined, the Egyptians must endure thirst, while the Hebrews drink amply:

> The cause
> of their torments
>
> was of benefit
> to those others . . . (11:13)

No names are named, as before. This is the delicacy of Sophia, and her precipitating irony as well. She knows who is meant, who stand in the circle of providence, and who are thrust outside.

Outside? but wait. Mercy is ample as water in the desert. Exodus knew nothing of the vast inclusive arm of God: yet here, awful Egypt is beckoned into the circle.

Sophia records it, for She is Providence. The Egyptians too

> . . . recognized
> the Lord (11:13)

✦   ✦   ✦

This was the word She gave Isaiah, this unprecedented turn and turn about. The pagan oppressor undergoes a change of heart, is transformed to a servant of Truth:

> When that day comes, there shall be an altar to the Lord
> in the heart of Egypt and a sacred pillar set up for the Lord
> upon her frontier.
>
> This shall stand as token and reminder to the Lord of Hosts
> in Egypt . . . (Isaiah 19:19)

More and more astonishing, the cycle: the omnipotent oppressor will taste the gall of oppression. Groaning for liberation, the people will be granted a new Moses, a prince of Egypt to sunder their chains:

> . . . so that when they appeal to Him against their oppres-
> sors, God may send a deliverer to champion their cause,
> and he shall rescue them (Isaiah 19:19–20)

✦   ✦   ✦

A second grief, and still no name.

But we know the name. We are to invoke it and grow wise in acknowl-edgment of our need. As we languish in a latter-day Egypt, an improbable liberator is named.

Then name the names, summon them!

Very well then: those of our lifetime who have rendered the enslaving edict null and void. Those who live as though the *pharaoh* and his "sys-tem" had little hold or none at all—on themselves, on us. The names of those who announce, with God's warrant, liberation is at hand.

The enablers, criminalized, endure scorn and prison. In passion of will and heart, they are free. And they set others free.

Unlikeliest of all: those who oppressed, imprisoned, tortured, disap-peared, the innocent ones.

Look to the original, and learn:

> The one whom they exposed
> to death,
> and afterward
> mockingly rejected—
>
> in the end
> they marveled at him (11:14)

✦ ✦ ✦

And again, we note nothing in Exodus of this outcome, this "marveling."

Yet another instructive midrash. It is as though Sophia summoned the principalities to judgment. And lo! in Her presence derision is transformed to dazed wonderment. The persecutors cry aloud: How wrong we were, how wrong!

Then. It is as though her glance, gentle and forthright, turned away from them. Turned in yearning compassion, to ourselves. She beholds the gallimaufry of the ages, even to our present millennium. And she urges: Look around you, here and now, and take heart.

And: Look within, and take heart!

✦ ✦ ✦

Judgment is rendered, but the matter is not done with.

We are puzzled. The mockery of the wicked turns to a kind of vertigo. And the pivot, the precipitation is this:

> The thirst
> they endured
>
> proved unlike
> that of the just (11:14)

We are back in Egypt, back in the Judean desert. Two peoples, two kinds of thirst, symbolic of opposed wills. The thirst of the wicked, and of the slave owners.

And the thirst of the just: an impassioned parching, tearing at the throat for—freedom now!

✦ ✦ ✦

11:15–16 Sophia takes circumstance strongly into account.

In everything, or at least in most things, moderation is the rule. This is the Wisdom of God.

Moderation, but not in everything. From fever to chills we are borne, the author veering from mood to mood, sometimes subtly, sometimes, as here, abruptly.

Those Egyptians: are they given over to idolatry? Wisdom stands (unwontedly?) in judgment. Beyond doubt these people are guilty. To wit: they worship crocodiles, snakes, lizards, scarabs.

✦   ✦   ✦

Ever the inspired moralist, Sophia is moved to offer another midrash. In view of a daring moral connection, She stretches the Exodus story to the limit. Her insight: the plagues that devastated Egypt are hardly to be thought an arbitrary punishment. Nor—and here surely we have a new wrinkle on the old parchment—are the plagues due to the obduracy of the pharaoh.

Not at all. What goes around, comes around: a rule of point. What is paid fealty turns on the idolaters, literally to plague them.

So, to our case. Worship of dumb serpents and worthless insects brings an onslaught of "senseless beasts" in retribution: frogs, gnats, flies, locusts.

✦   ✦   ✦

But Sophia knows too that punishment is morally useless, and at worst, damaging. The plagues are offered in a far different spirit: they are a merciless mercy, a drastic instruction. In their horrendous wake they bring awakening:

> to teach them
> that one is punished
>
> by the very things
> one sins by (11:16)

This is a hard saying: how then couch it, remove its implicit offense? For Sophia is ever mindful of the Greek-Hebrew mélange, a pressing matter of mutuality and noblesse oblige.

In tribute to present friendship, such words were best conveyed to ears absent—and ancient. Conveyed to those Egyptian slave masters, who presumably are no longer in position to hearken, or to recoil.

While the Greeks after all, are another matter: the host nation, very much present!

Nonetheless one notes that, biblically speaking, Sophia stands on firm ground:

> The one
> who conceived iniquity
>
> and was pregnant
> with mischief,
>
> brings forth failure (Psalm 7:15)

✦ ✦ ✦

Before me
they have dug a pit,

but they fall into it (Psalm 57:7)

✦ ✦ ✦

In arrogance they preferred
arrogance,

and like fools
they hated knowledge.

Now they must eat
the fruit
of their own way,

with their own devices
be glutted (Proverbs 1:30–31)

✦ ✦ ✦

And those Greeks: what, whom do they worship? Raising the question
would be the height of impropriety—if not of impudence. Nothing of that.

By any and all means, let these gracious hosts be held in honor—and
if perchance they take offense at the foregoing tale of Egyptian woes, let
them be appeased. Nothing, our author is aware, could be more apt to
calm ruffled egos than a reference to one of their own, their greatest own.

✦ ✦ ✦

11:17–19 *Dignum et justum*, then, is a nearly direct quote from the
Timaeus of sublime Plato: God (and be it noted, the omnipotent, omniscient God of the Hebrews, and introduced here almost as an
afterthought)—this God has "fashioned the universe from formless matter."

Sophia knows it: this fashioning God (Herself) could devise—anything.
Could devise a catastrophic flood, and the near end of things mortal. In
light of this acknowledgment, the plagues launched against Egypt were a
limited ill indeed, a kind of small-bore show of power.

What lightnings could she not have launched, this companionable
Angel turned Fury, were her destroying will allowed full play?

Why, She might have summoned a "newly created," apocalyptic
bestiary and released it against the oppressors. She could have harnessed
in a single onslaught, a squad of Greek and Hebrew confabulations: the
Gorgons and Medusa, the Chimera, teamed up with Leviathan, Behemoth.
Just imagine!

Sophia knows it: in spite of confounding provocation, God chose not to write "finis" to a human adventure gone woefully awry. Annihilation, extermination, a Last Day—what could have been launched—was not.

✦   ✦   ✦

Can we, amid the wreckage of the second millennium, conclude that provocation against the Divine ended, say, with the follies of Egypt?

Alas, later and far greater fools have arisen, rattling their weaponry, peddling across the world unimaginable follies.

Humans gone berserk threaten to launch "omnicide," a final blow against humans and creation. It stops the breath, it all but stops the heart: this provocation by human creatures, and the Creator withholding his hand. The patience of God, amid follies multiplied.

In a nuclear age, beasts more terrible than those contrived by ancient myths are "newly created" and roam abroad.

Amid a plague of cruise missiles and the rattling of nuclear arms, the pot valiance of ideologues and warriors, of liars and larcenists riding the cockpits of the nations—in such a world one must account the restraint of Sophia a singular mitigation and mercy.

✦   ✦   ✦

Is the world a loaded casino, where the wicked take all?

No, there is the love of God to be taken into account, to be rejoiced in. Sophia knows all things: She knows of that Love, to be celebrated in a later Scripture:

> Yes,
> God so loved the world
>
> as to give
> God's only Son
>
> that whoever
> believes in Him
>
> may not die. . . .

And the Gift is not withheld, though the world be Fallen, which is to say, given over to death.

Humans are torn this way and that with degradation and folly. Yet the Love endures, the Gift is given:

> The judgment
> of condemnation is this:
>
> the Light
> came into the world,

> but humans
> loved darkness
> rather than light
>
> because their deeds
> were wicked . . . (John 3:16, 19)

Shall Sophia set loose the hounds of hell, or shall she leash them close? We sense a kind of "restraining order" in effect: it is issued against a possibly (at times veering toward a probably)—a Final Act of God.

We believe it with all our beleaguered hearts: the order of withholding is issued by the prayer of the saints, the prophets and martyrs, the tortured and disappeared, those who perished in the gulags and extermination camps: poets and artists and rabbis and priests, parents and little children, Jesuits and gypsies; those who stood in the path of the hideous systems, those who said "no" in whatever way they could muster, against the ideology of contempt and death dealing.

By these the heart of Sophia is constrained, to withhold the thunders, the consequence.

✦   ✦   ✦

11:20 Through the holy ones, let us dare say (let us dare imagine, the image being our source of daring)—

> You have disposed
> all things
>
> by number,
> weight and measure . . .

"Weight and measure:" images of equity, justice, responsibility, as in Isaiah 28:17—

> I will make
> of right
>
> a measuring line,
>
> of justice,
> a level.

And again, in a sublime rhetorical question that implies its own answer:

> Who
> has cupped
> in hand

>   the waters
>   of the sea,
>
>   marked off
>   the heavens
>   with a span?
>
>   Who
>   has held
>   in a measure
>
>   the dust
>   of the earth?
>
>   weighed
>   the mountains
>   in scales?
>
>   and the hills
>   in a balance? (Isaiah 40:12)

Masterful author! The addition of "numbers" is a bow both subtle and courteous, in the direction of the Greek master, Pythagoras.

✦ ✦ ✦

11:21–26 Let us explore more closely the source of that "divine moderation" shown Egypt (shown Israel, shown Babylon, shown Assyria, shown Rome, shown America?)

First then to a confession of faith: the transcendent One, God, the Above and Beyond:

>   . . . great power
>   is always
>   at Your disposal.
>
>   Who can resist
>   the might
>   of Your arm? (11:21)

Then on, to images of right proportion—and this by confession of the true and lowly scope of created beings. Who are we, before God? Indeed, what is all creation?

The images suggest, even perhaps impel, a deflation of ego and illusion:

>   Before You
>   the entire world
>
>   is a speck of dust

> tilting
> a balance
> or a drop
> of morning dew
> come to earth (11:22)

✦ ✦ ✦

The deep heart of Sophia, conveying with artful simplicity ironies both disconcerting and healing!

> You have mercy
> on all
>
> because
> you can do
> all (11:23)

A statement baldly, even roughly put: but what soundless depth it plumbs!

The Omnipotent, Who by reason of that power, in the clashing and joining of opposites, is the all Merciful.

Sophia, God. God, Sophia. The ever Beyond, Who nevertheless, in an act of sublime courtesy, bends to us:

> You close Your eyes
> to sin,
>
> that the sinner
> may repent (11:23)

It is all finally quite simple. What She has created, Sophia laves in an aura of love. Hatred, alienation, reprisal—these are foreign to Her heart, the heart of all:

> You love
> all things
> that are:
>
> nothing
> of creation
> do You find loathsome.
>
> For
> what You hated
>
> You would not have fashioned (11:24)

BJ notes well: The thought of these verses is not new to the Bible. But never has it been stated with such force and serenity.

Nor elsewhere, with so persuasive a justification.

✦   ✦   ✦

In the week of Genesis, Love set all in motion. Then in a continuing mystery, the initial act is extended.

The "big bang" becomes biography. Creation, then duration. All beings enter (and create as they come), history:

> How
> could anything
>
> remain
> in existence
>
> unless
> You willed it:
>
> or
> be preserved
>
> had You not
> called it forth? (11:25)

The conclusion is prodigious, sublime:
You spare all things

> because
> they are Yours,
>
> O Lord and Lover of life!
>
> You
>
> Whose imperishable Breath
> dwells in all! (11:26)

It is like the sounding paean of Gerard Manley Hopkins:

> Yet did the dark side of the bay of thy blessing
> Not vault them, the millions of rounds of thy mercy not
> reeve even them in? . . . ("The Wreck of the Deutschland")

✦   ✦   ✦

12:1–2 That "imperishable Breath" is celebrated as the *élan vital* of all beginnings (Genesis 2:7).

The psalmist too takes up the theme, but with a difference. Now we celebrate a Pentecostal "second Sending":

> When You
> send forth
> Your Spirit
>
> they are created,
> and You

renew
the face of the earth (Psalm 105:30)

Job, for his part, will equate his own life with this Breath. He breathes It, therefore he is. It is the Breath of his being, his soul's respiration.

And more: the Spirit is Enabler and Guarantor: through Her, the afflicted holy one speaks the truth (27:3):

So long as I
have life in me,

and the Breath of God
dwells

in my nostrils—

my lips
shall not
speak falsehood

nor my tongue
utter deceit!

How rich and varied is this Respiration, how manifold the Gifts of the Spirit!

✦ ✦ ✦

And what of sinners—which is to say, ourselves? Paul offers a salutary reminder, and a reproof as well:

Do you presume on God's kindness and forbearance? Do you not know that God's kindness is an invitation to you, to repent? (Romans 2:4)

✦ ✦ ✦

As for Sophia, how does she regard sinners, how treat with them? Paul's threat of brimstone is entirely absent. And we are reassured:

Little by little
You rebuke sinners,

warn them,

remind them
of defaults

that they
may turn from evil

and believe in You,
O Lord! (12:2)

She is the spirit of Jesus, all said:

Who among you,
if he has a hundred sheep
and loses one,

does not leave the ninety-nine
in the wilderness

and follow the lost one
until he find it?

And when he finds it,
he puts it to shoulder
in jubilation . . .

I tell you

there will be
more joy in heaven
for one repentant sinner

than over ninety-nine righteous
who have no need
to repent (Luke 15:4–5, 7)

✦   ✦   ✦

12:3–5 Sophia turns to history (to what might be termed revisionist history), and offers an instance of divine clemency. Of mercy, though beyond doubt limited.

The conquest of Canaan: many hands and minds have labored over the complex saga. Many versions, governed by various ideologies, survive—puzzling, intriguing, stopping us short.

The traditions veer about wildly. One speaks of a quick war, exterminating those who oppose the God's will. Another version describes a gradual takeover and assimilation.

Here, Sophia lingers over one episode, a curious one. The tale of the wasps is borrowed from Exodus 23:28. These forerunning stingers are, as presented, a species of barbed mercy. They "exterminate by degrees."

Their stings were not immediately or necessarily fatal. So, fleeing the horde, tribal sinners gained time. The reasoning:
Condemning them
bit by bit,

> You
> gave them space
> for repentance (12:2)

Worse could have befallen, far worse: an exterminating bolt from on high, or an onslaught by wild animals:

> Not
> that it was impossible
>
> to vanquish the wicked
> in battle
> against the just
>
> or wipe them out
> at a single blow
>
> by terrible beasts,
>
> or by one
> decisive word . . .

We are hardly reassured by the omnipotent flexing, this mulling over ways and means of punishment. And we reflect ruefully: this ancient deity of Exodus, his (sic) actions laced with anger and a will bent on vengeance—how hard he dies in the mind, how perduring those themes of divine recrimination!

Why, we wonder, this justification of awful events? It is hardly to be accounted an echo of Sophia's compassion, so recently sounding in the text:

> You
> have mercy on all . . .
>
> You
> love all things
> that are. . . .
>
> You
> spare all,
>
> because
> they are yours . . .
>
> Now, another tone, a wintry blast for sure:
> these ancient inhabitants
> of your holy land,
>
> whom you hated
>
> for deeds
> most odious . . .

The deeds are horrendous, and cataloged in gruesome detail. But to whom are the brutish practices to be imputed? Who are responsible?

Notably, the reference to "orgies . . . bloody banquets" indicts, not the ancient Canaanites, but rites current among mystery religions, in the Greece of the diaspora.

The offenses are contemporary with the Greek-Hebrew scene: thus the highly oblique reference.

Too close for comfort?

✦   ✦   ✦

The indictment continues: it charges cannibalism and infanticide.

We, for our part, are set back. The former crime is unattested elsewhere against the Canaanites. As to the latter, we note that the slaying of infants was hardly unheard of in Israel itself.

Recounting one domestic episode, it is as though the chronicler of 1 Kings cannot bear to speak directly. He chooses instead a concealing euphemism:

> During his reign, Hiel from Bethel rebuilt Jerico. He lost his first-born son, Abiram, when he laid the foundation, and his youngest son, Segub, when he set up the gates . . . (16:34)

The psalmist also testifies:

We have sinned,

we
and our fathers:

we
have committed crimes:
have done wrong. . . .

They sacrificed
sons and daughters,
to demons:

they shed innocent blood,
the blood
of sons and daughters . . . (106:6, 37–38)

✦　✦　✦

Has Sophia regressed? In the account of the conquest (book of Numbers), we have seen it before: the creating of scapegoats, the sidestepping from responsibility. Guilt is adduced, blame falls—and always elsewhere. On Canaanites anciently: here even on Greeks.

Concomitantly, a fictive history of Jewish innocence is woven whole cloth. The awful wars of conquest and extermination are cleansed of crime.

And perhaps most striking of all is the contravention, deific and horrific, both. The One to Whom visionaries and prophets testify, God of nonviolence, Advocate of the victimized—we can scarce credit our eyes—this One is purged from the text.

Beyond doubt, in the years of the Canaanite wars, the God of the prophets would have stood with the victims, on whatever side they fell.

And our text. Has the God of Ezekiel been twice exiled, has Wisdom fled the earth? An ancient deity, fiery and uncontrollably violent, is rehabilitated. He (sic) prods the wars forward, announces them as jihads, matters of high virtue, of his will.

✦　✦　✦

12:6–7 After Isaiah and the other sublime spirits, we thought to have done with such a god.

And we were wrong. The old god is alive, resurrected and here addressed. No more of tender Sophia, no more the God of Wisdom. To the eye of the author, the deity of *sturm und drag* is at large, alert—and spoiling for battle.

That fierce shadowy presence! He pushes swords, hot from the forge of Mars, into the hands of true believers. And the chronicler leaves no room for doubt: Canaanites will pay dear.

You willed
to destroy (them)

by the hands
of our fathers,

that the land
dearest of all
to you,

might receive

a worthy colony
of God's children.

The chauvinism stops the breath. So does the word *colony*, that bow in the direction of Greek hosts, in gratitude for a welcome accorded.

✦   ✦   ✦

And a question, an urgent one. Why this sea change in our author? A few verses ago were we not rejoicing, led as we were, verse by vibrant verse, toward the heart of God?

On a vexing matter, learned commentators are silent. No speculation or puzzlement. It is as if the Word were set in adamant on the page, to be taken in stride. No critique, no summoning of second (or third) thoughts.

And yet, a sudden discordant ringing of changes, so clamorous we are tempted to cover our ears.

Could there be an intent at work here, latent, subtle, a fuse joined to a light? Let us strike it.

The text turns about. It bespeaks a rupture in common understanding, in social sensibility.

A hint of the fateful ease with which a people, including Christian people (perhaps we foremost), turn aside from a clear example and its exemplar. Turn and twist and at all cost indulge a game of sterile logic, justifying thereby, a murderous military adventuring.

Christian history thus verifies painfully the truth of the text. The ease with which we summon a pantheon of atavists, the gods of war.

Regression, temptation yielded to, in aggravation of spirit, or a lust well concealed, for advantage, control, domination.

✦   ✦   ✦

We note too the distortion and infection of memory that follow on war making. Memories of conquest, of "victory," create their own fictions, fictions people live by, kill for, die for, again and again. Fictions that spawn illusions, illusions that urge "another try," or "a war to end all wars," or some such nonsense.

And the wars create fictive gods as well, deities both suitable and advantageous, gods favoring our dark design of domination and prospering.

✦   ✦   ✦

Today the discordant changes of our text are rung once more, loud and clear. What we would become in virtue of Bible and tradition must encounter our woeful behavior in the world. What a clash, what incoherence and self-deception! No stopping our ears, no willing the fearful imbalance out of existence.

✦   ✦   ✦

And a chastened gratitude is due our author. Painfully he reminds us: the Hebrew conquest and today's welter of wars—these are a like awful game.

Then as now, glorious Sophia is stripped, humiliated, exiled, raped, tortured, disappeared. The text is snatched from her, she has lost her place of honor in hearts and minds. In a Fallen world, such as She can win no fealty.

In dark times she must contend (we must contend) with the shadowy principalities. They forge and champion the sword, that mighty persuader.

Those forces! To them death, in all its metaphors, is a prime, indeed a sole social good. Whose gods are armed, who would have us so bedizened, in their image.

✦   ✦   ✦

12:12–18 We begin a review of the incompatibles with which Job wrestled—and took a fall.

Will this wise one, we wonder, fare better against an omnipotent Adversary? We must salute courage, if not temerity.

Job's own question enters the text. But with a difference.

> Who can say
> to Him:
>
> "What
> are you doing?" (9:12)

Our author moves close, face to face with the Deity, a "Thou":

> Who can say
> to You:
>
> "What have you done?"

> Or who oppose
> Your decree? (Wisdom 12:12)

Power and mercy, omnipotence and compassion: do these coexist in God? Yes, we are assured, for God is—God.

But does a suspicion linger? Does the assured response, its speedy utterance, its unshadowed nimbus, bespeak a nimble accommodation?

How we strain and wrench the cables of faith, grasping to hold on, somehow!

We stand within history, that volcanic hot spot. At the verge—what anomalies, ironies, oppositions!

How many have fallen over the seething cusp, and perished.

No denying it, another image: believers are stretched on a procrustean bed:

> Who
> justly cites
> You
>
> for crushing a people
> You
> have created?
>
> Who comes
> into Your presence,
>
> vindicating
> the unjust? (12:12)

We are on familiar ground. Is it a quicksand?

Indeed this God ordains all things sweetly—or bitterly. But sweet or sour the decree—no one, not just Job in all his withheld glory, shall summon God to explain or justify.

Wisdom, so to speak, is wisely silent. Let the wise learn of Her. Learn silence.

God judges: God is not to be judged.

> No,
> besides You
> there is no god.
>
> You
> have care
> of all.
>
> To show
> such a one

> that your judgments
> are not unjust—
>
> of this
>
> You
> have no need (12:13)

The daring of this neo-Job! Again and again, he ventures to tell God who God is. And unprecedented is this too: for many a verse—our author being eloquent if not verbose—from on high comes neither interruption nor constraint.

Does silence signify agreement?

Wonder of wonders, this (chancy?) version of the Ineffable is received, as far as can be judged, with satisfaction. The message of silence being: who God is—you are free to tell.

The author dares go further. By implication, he instructs God in godly ways. It is done with ease and finesse, under guise of an elegant strophe of praise:

> Just
> You are,
>
> You
> govern all justly.
>
> To condemn the innocent
> You regard
>
> as unworthy
> of Your power (12:15)

Just governance coupled with compassion: another expression of the challenge offered by grace to gravity.

The balancing act continues, a high wire act of the mind. Such daring! It mimes the divine lightness of being.

The word of God concerning God. We are astonished, startled, raised on high:

> Master of might,
>
> You
> judge
>
> with clemency.
>
> With leniency
> You
> govern us.

You
have but to will it,

and Your power
is there (12:18)

✦ ✦ ✦

12:19–21 We are led through an ancient theme, the divine favor shown a few, severity toward the many, the outsiders.

And in this harping, one thinks, Wisdom shows herself somewhat less than wise: at the least, atavistic. Her god is pleased merely and lightly to "correct" the chosen.

To these favored, the god proves vastly comforting—as well as useful. And the "enemies?" Them the god destroys. The "perverse" are condemned out of hand.

There follows in this dark logic, a mortal threat against life and land.

✦ ✦ ✦

A question persists. In the story of the Canaan conquest, does mirror meet mirror, god reflect god? Can it be (cold comfort to the chosen), that the goys too have gods at beck and nod, deities both pugnacious and obeisant?

✦ ✦ ✦

The text is down putting indeed. Still, we take heart.

Long before, an atavistic "wisdom" has been mightily surpassed. We have learned from Isaiah of a God of universal forbearance. The walls are down, the prophet declared thunderously: tribal religion is ousted, in favor of all. To be created is to be summoned: all are chosen, all beckoned into the light.

✦ ✦ ✦

12:22 "We," and "they." What a persistent, pernicious rupture of communality! And all sanctioned by this god. who one thinks, embarrassingly resembles the "chosen"—here self-confessed as sinful.

According to the Talmud, their sin is this: they separate what should be joined.

There is a lofty, Shakespearian tone to the passage. It is as though the words, balanced, nuanced, juridical, were pronounced from a throne. From Solomon's throne, to be sure:

Us
you chastise:
our enemies
with a thousand blows
you punish—

so that
when we judge,

we may recall
your goodness:

and
being judged,

may look for mercy.

✦   ✦   ✦

12:23–27 The idea recurs (from 11:16): misuse or abuse of creation brings punishment.

First, the delinquents are dealt with as infants, misbehaving innocents. Their offense is slight, so a slight chastisement befits—a mere tap of the wrist, so to speak. But if the love tap proves of no avail? Then set loose a barrage "worthy of god"—or of Jupiter perhaps! A legion of thunderbolts.

✦   ✦   ✦

The divorce syndrome is in full play.

The verses are a moralistic recalling of the Egyptian servitude. Then, social classes of slave master and slave dramatized the "separation of that which should be joined." A state of sin: to be sure, of Egyptian sin.

But wait. Recalling those years, their shame, can by no means heal the separation.

Hatred is fanned once more, torrid. The exclusion is drastic. Even in memory, at the remove of centuries, nothing of history is healed.

The god too remembers, the wound of the god festers.

The mirror image again?

Or this: it is as though the maleficent "we" and "they" are held aloft, an amputated head and a headless corpse.

✦   ✦   ✦

Dignum et justum it was, fitting and just that "they" were condignly punished, in the death of their firstborn. Had they not decreed the death of our firstborn?

And let their armies be exterminated in the sea. Did they not seek in a hundred shameful decrees, our downfall?

✦ ✦ ✦

Another millennium dawns as these notes are set down. And the ancient logic holds fast, in heaven as on earth.

Our gods are said to dwell on high: in fact they are rooted in the dank soil of our hearts, parasites and prisoners of our Fallen estate. They continue to speak for us, as we for them.

And in a logic forged in hell—should not the enemy of our gods, be our enemy as well?

We, they . . . Bloody tit for tat!

✦ ✦ ✦

"Wisdom" here, fiercely atavistic, belies her name and her earlier, lofty instruction. It is as though creation is being destroyed by a voracious, advancing black hole. Sophia is drawn back and back, she cries aloud in ancestral fury, hardly surpassing the vile morality implicit in much of Exodus.

What, we ask, of the sublime teaching, the marvels of insight and intuition that went before?

✦ ✦ ✦

The verses imply an outpouring of questions.

Why this fierce counter to herself? Would Sophia have us know her failings, which so curiously resemble our own? Does she appear as Unwisdom, that we might learn our follies? Does she come toward us as a vindictive Fury, punishing the "outsiders," that we might turn to mercy, through One who dissolves all boundaries?

Shall we come to a chastened sense of limits, knowing that Sophia is no endowment of ours, available on call—but the utterly Other, the gift of God, freely given or sternly withheld?

Too, might we also come to know the Fall—the Fall in us, the Fall of this day, this hour? Might know the Unwisdom that clothes us in fictive rags of justification, a show of credential in hand, lines drawn, rancor and enmities, "we" and "they," wars that breed and bring forth—wars?

chapter eight

Nature worship and idolatry: "no vision, nor ears to hear, nor fingers for feeling . . ." (13:1–15:19)

13:1–3 Wisdom stands before all creation, all generations, and demands to be known, to be paid fealty. Well and good.

Except that—we are who we are, through all generations. The Fallen tribe.

Majestic, veiled, Her Presence is concealed within the scrim of visible creation.

And we? We see nothing, we turn away, veer off the sure way, lost, unknowing (or uncaring) of our loss.

She knows. She tells. The forked road, the detours, the multiple ways of going—nowhere.

✦ ✦ ✦

The first illusive way is the Route of Appearances. Many go that way, the way of beauty, commanding the heart's veneration.

Wisdom lists the signs, awesome and enticing, that lead humans awry:

> Fire,
> or wind,
>
> or swift air,
> or circuit of the stars,
>
> or mighty waters,
> or luminaries of heaven—
>
> these
> they venerated
> as gods,
>
> as governors
> of the world! (13:2)

Following Plato, the Stoics saw in veneration of the stars and the forces of nature, the origin of Greek deities. Astrology gave a new impetus to the cult of the astral bodies, those "governors of the world."

With all this, Sophia is lenient. She knows the human heart, how the

147

majesty and beauty of creation hold us enchanted. Granting that seduc-
tion, she keeps her counsel. The truth is her guiding star.

How greatly She surpasses all the works of Her hands:

> Now if,
> charmed by beauty,
>
> they saw in such things
> very gods—
>
> let them know
> how far more excellent
> is the Creator.
>
> For
> it is the Artisan
> of beauty itself
>
> Who
> brought them forth (13:3)

Whatever the golden Greek eye lingers over, and transforms—Wisdom
too lingers over, and how lovingly! She knows, she concedes—the nimbus
of high culture. How easily we give ourselves to that which in plenary
measure gives itself to us: the intoxication, the wine cup of creation raised
on high.

✦   ✦   ✦

The instruction will be more easily heard, if Her sympathy is manifest.

13:4–9 In this wise. Wisdom too knows the sweet folly of the senses:
sweet indeed, but folly:

> If
> they are struck
>
> by the mighty
> energy of things,
>
> only
> let them realize
>
> how much more powerful
>
> is the One
> who made them (13:4)

The Greeks are favored in every arena: in intellect, intuition, in literary, philosophical, and dramatic genius. The life of the mind glows like a
jewel that owns the sun, like a star that goes before, leading the wise.

By all means, let them follow, search on, penetrate further the reality
that so enchants them:

> From
> the greatness and beauty
> of created things,
>
> their original Author,
> by analogy
> is seen (13:5)

Her heart dilates with compassion for those who, amid the glories of creation, stop short of the Creator:

> For these,
>
> blame
> is light:
>
> they have perhaps
> gone astray
>
> though
> they seek God
>
> and long
> to find Her (13:6)

Does She see evidence of this "adoration of appearances" among Greek poets and philosophers? It would seem so:

> Inquiring deeply
> among God's works,
>
> they are distracted
> by what they see—
>
> so beautiful it is! (13:7)

Vast is the contribution, and unto all generations, of these creative artists, sculptors, poets, magicians of the mind.

Still, for all their eminence, Sophia is clear. They do not escape judgment:

> No,
> not even these
>
> are pardonable!
>
> for
> if they acquired
> such vast knowledge
>
> ranging,
> scrutinizing
> the universe itself—

> how came it, they
> did not
>
> the more promptly
> discover Sophia? (13:8–9)

This is *parti pris,* one thinks, with a vengeance.

In such severity, is the Sophia of our book to be thought the somber forerunner of Paul's Letter to the Romans, with its devastating judgment against the pagans?

In that vast interdiction, what are we to conclude concerning Buddhists and Hindus and Moslems and others—of our own day, of olden days, those martyrs and confessors of other faiths who stand beside the holiest of our own?

This summons issued to the Greeks, to judgment, even mild judgment—one finds it perplexing, even down-putting, the lapse of a generous spirit.

Worse is to follow. The Greeks, along with others, have worshipped not only the forces of nature: they have dared fashion idols.

This is literally damnable. Or so Sophia declares, Pauline to the hilt.

✦   ✦   ✦

13:10 A glare of brimstone is shortly to descend.

In its light, the preceding must be accounted an ever so slight rumble in the heavens.

Those who worship cosmic "divinities" are, as we have noted, hosts of the Hebrews. They include the preeminent artists and intellects of the world, an elite unmatched. Is it not prudent then of our author and moralist to tread lightly? It is.

✦   ✦   ✦

Those (Greeks) who bow to the powers of nature and the heavens are accounted merely "vain," and easily forgiven. Sophia could turn a benign eye on these, conceding that the "forces" so worshipped are hardly to be dismissed as dead "works of their hands." No, these powers possess "might and energy": they are even in a sense beneficent.

✦   ✦   ✦

But now, beware: a great crime remains in place, yet to be indicted. Name it, the abomination. Some among the Greeks, like their neighbors, dare contrive—idols.

Sun worshippers are merely "vain." But these, whether pagans or Hebrew renegades, are nothing short of "accursed." And are thus stigmatized.

Pen or sword? Occasion warranting, Sophia wields the one like the other.

And Hers is no diatribe in a vacuum. Upon some of the indicted, disaster has already fallen. Jews have proven faithless, bowing to sticks and stones. Amid this crisis the polemic of Sophia is launched.

✦ ✦ ✦

The Greeks are by no means the first threat against Hebrew faith. From of old, the time of the Exodus, the brusque inveighing of Sophia has ample warrant.

✦ ✦ ✦

And the idolatry of "the nations," as well as of "the chosen," as well as of the churches, continues. A sordid evidence that the Fall had perdured.

How unmask the idolatries, how translate original forms into current reality, that consciences be enlightened? A daunting task.

Neglected or ignored, our text is reduced to a fainéant folklore.

What can it mean to such as ourselves, as the twenty-first century rolls on?

Eons ago, the unenlightened hewed or cast images of their gods, and prostrated before them. Today, the self-justifying clichés multiply: we of a more enlightened age admit of no idols in our homes, workplaces, malls, streets, churches, etc., etc.

Then we pause: Wisdom would have us grow thoughtful. Technological idolatry skillfully conceals its true nature—and this most cleverly through its fabricators and justifiers.

The level of concealment, and more—of denial—on the part of politicians, engineers, research scientists, media, is stupefying.

Thus an ethically outrageous, indeed demented project—mass destruction of humans, havoc against the ecology—this is presented straight-faced, with a brawny logic, as legitimate, necessary, protective. The abnormal is normalized. The gods of death clutter the landscape, coast to coast: factories, research centers, silos and bunkers, airstrips, naval bases. Tourists visit the Pentagon and its prayer room, where national and religious holidays are celebrated, and Bible study groups assemble.

A few have striven in the last decades to unmask the nuclear idols, entering their shrines, pouring blood on the weapons, wielding household hammers in accord with the word of Isaiah: swords into plowshares.

✦ ✦ ✦

In the early morning hours of December 19, 1999, Philip Berrigan, Susan Crane, Rev. Stephen Kelly, S.J., and Elizabeth Walz, calling themselves the PLOWSHARES VS. DEPLETED URANIUM, disarmed two A-10 Thunderbolt bombers (also known as Warthogs) at the Warfield Air National Guard facility in Essex, Maryland.

They were arrested at the base by federal air police. The four had worked on the bombers, hammering on the Gatling gun and on the pylons under the wings, and pouring their blood into the engines. They hung banners on the site and left a large rosary hanging over the Gatling . . .

An A-10 is an aircraft built around a gun—a Gatling that can spew 3,900 rounds per minute. This criminal plane fired 95 percent of the depleted uranium deployed by the U.S. since the Gulf War, leaving behind 300 to 800 tons, poisoning humans and the elements of Kuwait and Iraq.

Sanctions (a crime against humanity) and depleted uranium (a war crime) have killed 2 million Iraquis since the war's end . . . .

✦   ✦   ✦

In courtrooms, events that follow are hammered in stone.

The justice system colludes closely with the idols, the gods of the A-10 and their uranium-tipped monsters. Judges and prosecutors unroll a peremptory apparatus to justify these inordinate systems of death.

Evidence brought forward by the defendants is sternly restricted. International law, conscience, the Bible, motivation, are declared irrelevant. A juridical mask descends on the artificers of mass killing, and on their handiwork.

Shortly, Susan, Stephen, Elizabeth, and Philip are criminalized and convicted. Found guilty of "destroying government property," "weakening national security," and similar absurd charges.

As transpired, the text of the trial and its outcome are certain as tomorrow becoming today:

> (Tuesday, March 14, 2000) Judge James Smith denied yesterday a request by the four defendants to allow experts to testify at their trial . . . on laws regarding the use of depleted uranium in military weapons.

> (Friday, March 24, 2000). Judge James Smith ignored a prosecutor's suggested guidelines and imposed stiff prison sentences on longtime peace activist Philip Berrigan, and three codefendants, charged with malicious destruction of . . . warplanes.

✦   ✦   ✦

Thus with a sharp blow of the gavel, the lesson is driven home: the public *cultus*, the official religion of the empire, is nuclear idolatry. *In Hoc*

Signo Vinces (in this sign you shall overcome): not "the sign of" the non-violent, crucified Christ, to be sure.

And the public lends its assent by a collusive indifference. Society, economy, polity are organized in favor of the idols, and the unarguable supposition of their beneficial character.

✦ ✦ ✦

There is however a rub—though to the imperial eye, a slight one, and easily ignored.

The rub? Sophia objects. And in most unaccustomed terms, this nurturing, forgiving Being. Her denunciation is strenuous, furious. She borrows the voice of a fiery Hecuba, a Cassandra:

> Doomed
> are they
>
> and
> in dead things
> lie their hopes
>
> who term as gods,
>
> mere things
> made
> by human hands (13:10)

13:11–19 The contempt is palpable. Sophia borrows whole cloth a parable from great Isaiah (44:9–20). Thus she mimes the horrific contradictions that govern the idolaters.

Simultaneous, unapprehended, they put creation to right use—and to overt misuse. Isaiah and Sophia are agreed: the artisan of idols is morally schizophrenic. Isaiah:

> With part of the wood
> he warms himself
>
> or makes a fire
> for baking bread
>
> But then—his mind is distracted, he is put to shame:
> Of what remains,
> he makes a god,
> his idol,
>
> and prostrates
> before it
>
> in worship.
>
> He implores an "it":

"Rescue me,
for you are my god."

Wonderfully vivid, lucid, to the point, a moral commentary follows.
First, Isaiah proposes an ironic interior monologue.

Proposes: and then with added force, he laments the absence of moral reflection. Such is declared impossible to the delinquent: it is left for the prophet to set matters right. This rueful denuded artisan does not reflect or have intelligence and sense to say:

Half the wood
I burned in the fire,

and on its embers
I baked bread

and roasted meat
which I ate.

shall I then
out of the rest,
make an abomination

or worship
a block of wood?

The improbable monologue winds down to a moral conclusion, a flat judgment:

He
is chasing ashes,
a thing

that cannot save itself
when the flame consumes it.

Yet he does not say:

This thing
in my right hand

is a fraud.

✦   ✦   ✦

Sophia's diatribe is similar in outline, but her contempt is even more palpable. She refuses the idolater the dignity of worthwhile material or work. His wood is a "good for nothing refuse from remnants": it is "crooked, full of knots."

And his product, the image? It is indifferently done, he "listlessly whiles away an idle hour."

"With red stain" he "daubs over the blemishes."

A final indignity accrues to artisan and image. And to a duped mind, the insult goes unperceived:

> For his image
>
> he makes
> a fitting shrine:
>
> fastens it
> to the wall
> with a nail.
>
> Thus
> lest it fall,
> he provides a place,
>
> knowing full well
> its helplessness (13:15–16)

Knowing and not knowing. If he knew, how could he bring himself to bow and scrape before a dead stick? He has yielded to irrationality.

Sophia spells it out with devastating, detailed rhetoric, very Greek in tone.

Imagine! He brings to the idol his serious concerns: "his goods . . . marriage . . . children."

All in vain, all to his shame.

> For vigor,
>
> he invokes
> the powerless.
> For his life . . .
> the dead.
>
> For aid . . .
> the wholly incompetent.
>
> For his travels . . .
> something
> stuck in place.
>
> For profit
> in business,
>
> for success
> with his hands—
>
> its hands
> completely inert (13:18–19)

✦ ✦ ✦

Inescapable, the conclusion. Sophia leads believers to the cross. It is that simple, that austere. To the cross.

✦ ✦ ✦

Given the human plight today, the truth is of supreme moment. Our predicament goes by many names: nuclear arsenal, consumerism, racism—socialized, institutional idolatries.

Another: the "School of the Americas" in Fort Benning, Georgia. There for a generation, North Americans have been training the vilest despots of Latin America in the niceties of their trade, including torture and the slaughter of peasants, nuns, and priests.

But for Unwisdom, let the Catholic chaplain of Fort Benning be heard from:

> Speaking by phone . . . the chaplain said his parish council has included former SOA faculty members and its chief of staff.
>
> "These are just profoundly decent, committed lay men and women who would have nothing to do with a place that was doing something tawdry or wrong or immoral," he said.
>
> (Catholic News Service, 6/25/1999)

"Good Germans," and their "good priest"?

✦ ✦ ✦

Repeatedly we see the evidence: idolatry as a national religion. The idols are folded neatly into nature, anchored to the landscape, landmarks of national consciousness.

Culture, economy, military muscle, death rows, and abortion clinics—it all coheres in a kind of "second nature," close woven, intact: death on demand.

Nuclearism is our religion. And the law of the land justifies the arrangement.

Are there objections? A "justice system" is in place. As these notes are set down, our nearest and dearest are in prison. Thus a lifeline is woven, and a gentle instruction implied.

✦ ✦ ✦

This is the wisdom of the world, nuclear idolatry.

It stands as a beacon of despair, it sinks deep as a continental plate.

It exists in utter contravention to the wisdom of Sophia, and of the cross.
Sophia has encountered Greek wisdom, and declared a better.
So, later, does Paul:

> Has not God turned the wisdom of this world into folly?
>
> In God's wisdom the world did not come to know God through "wisdom." It pleased God to save those who believe through the absurdity of the preaching of the gospel.
>
> Yes, Jews demand "signs," Greeks look for "wisdom." But we preach Christ crucified—a stumbling block to Jews, an absurdity to gentiles.
>
> But to those who are called, Jews and Greeks alike, Christ the power of God and the wisdom of God.
>
> For God's folly is wiser than humans, and His weakness more powerful (1 Corinthians 1:21–25)

✦　✦　✦

In Hoc Signo Vinces (in this sign, you shall overcome). The vision was a turning point, a hinge of history.

The hinge turned in its socket: it turned wrong. The "Constantinian arrangement" followed. It implied the acceptance of worldly wisdom at its apogee: armed force below, blessing from on high. And Christianity

reverted with shocking speed to the Hebrew god and his avenging armies.

Blessing from on high? We had in our scripture a hint of an earlier grace, accorded the apostle Thomas:

> Blessed are those
> who have not seen,
>
> and have believed.

Constantine, true to the wisdom of the mighty, misread the sign on high. And the Church also read the sign wrong, and so passed from "believing" to purported "seeing."

The wisdom of God, so often misread by us humans! The Cross appeared in the heavens: so goes the tradition. The epiphany was an ultimate urging to forsake arms and armed might. To embrace nonviolence, the "folly" of which Paul wrote.

But emperors are generally illiterate in matters that threaten their close interests. They bring, even to a vision on high, a blurring scrim of suppositions. They wear a crown, they wield a scepter, they wear a sword—mighty instruments of decoding.

A voice urges: "It must mean this . . ." and "surely it could not mean that . . ."

To interpret the vision, to bend it to the king's sway, a priesthood, we may surmise, was at hand. And prophets were not.

The priests were useful, which is to say, they too were ethically illiterate.

So the intent of heaven was frustrated. The vision of the Cross was turned around: symbol and message became a magical totem, a *vexilla regis,* woven in a banner and its monstrous motto.

Thereupon the emblem was borne into battle, the standard of imperial might. God being for us, who shall oppose?

✦   ✦   ✦

Thus a far different history supervened: the pursuit of worldly wisdom, a path of tears and blood.

And a former way was lost: the way of Sophia of the Cross.

✦   ✦   ✦

14:1–7 Another instance of worship accursed. And again, the contempt boils on the page.

For sake of gain, someone embarks on a wild voyage. At the prow of the ship is a carved image. All on board

cry out
to a hunk of wood

more unsound

than the boat
that bears them (14:1).

Greed funded the boat. A kind of artisan "wisdom" (the word is deliciously ironic) fashioned it, together with its protective image at the prow.

Some wisdom, this simulacrum! is the implication of Sophia. The wooden image is vain: it cannot speed the ship safely on its way. That task is left to "Your Providence"—an extraordinary title, in the Septuagint only found here. And we have Greek literature to thank for the expression.

Providence is active on all sides, according to large-hearted Sophia. Imagine! even inexperienced seamen and traders may embark with confidence, once "Your Providence" has been invoked.

"You": no longer "it" or "they," but the direct address of faithful prayer.

Your Wisdom

is not to remain
idle or sterile

Wisdom declares it, deliciously.

The Greeks, we note, were great seamen and traders. To the eye of Sophia, their daring merits an encomium, a bow of admiration. So be it then: fittingly, the riches of foreign lands and the seas surrounding are drawn in and in, as though with vast nets.

✦　✦　✦

Cunning Sophia, leading the mind beyond expectation.

The foregoing argument, pitting Providence versus the idols, is by way of historical prelude.

Then on, to this immemorial tale. Anciently, it was the time of the downfall of the race of proud giants. And as everyone knows, the story passed on and on, of a "frail skiff" built under divine command.

(Frail? a mere skiff? Its dimensions, we learn (Genesis 6:15) were a formidable 440 feet by 73 by 44!)

In any case, into the ark trod an irreplaceable treasure, fauna, humans, two by two, "the hope of the universe."

The waters rose: now the boat was afloat. Willy nilly, all aboard shortly must endure a raging flood tide, forty days and nights of storm, submerging all creation.

And what relief to know that against monstrous odds of nature, the ark prevailed. Safe it came to port, a sprightly survivor, sound in seam and timber. Thus earning a blessing, here delightfully appended:

> blessed
> the wood
>
> which serves
> the cause
> of justice (14:7)

✦   ✦   ✦

14:8–10 For every blessing, a curse. Here, a brisk denunciation against the misuse of wood—an idol serving injustice. Sophia announces the woe:

> Cursed
> be the idol
>
> which issues
> from human hands—
>
> accursed
> the idol,
>
> accursed
> its artisan.

✦   ✦   ✦

14:11 By implication, the foregoing judgment fell primarily on renegade Jews. But the "nations" and their gods are hardly spared: they too "amid God's creation" are an "abomination," a "snare," a "trap." The fierce terms must be thought to indict among others, Greeks and their religious rites.

Sophia, undiplomatic, stern? Indeed yes, when the truth is at stake.

✦   ✦   ✦

14:12–21 On to the origins of idolatry. It sprang, we are told, from a kind of "fornication."

The covenant, we recall, was presented again and again under the sign of a marriage between Sophia and the chosen. When idols were contrived, a vow was violated. And the idolaters are here judged: adulterers, prostitutes, fornicators.

Still, a large hope remains:

> In
> the beginning
>
> idols
> were not:

nor
shall they continue
forever,

for

by human vanity

they entered the world . . . (14:13–14)

Sophia and the author of Genesis are at one: true God is author of time and this world. Only later, after the Fall (and beyond doubt due to that catastrophe), polytheism laid claim to the human clan.

For awhile only, the idols plague us: therefore a brusque end is their destiny.

The word *vanity* is of note—the fault which fuels the idols. (Webster: "Quality of being vain, futile, worthless, idle. Being excessively proud of oneself or one's qualities")

One thinks: the imperial fault par excellence.

✦ ✦ ✦

Theories abound as to the origins. Sophia sums up two of these:

Humans,

victimized
by loss

or by the power
of rulers,

conferred

on stocks and stones

the incommunicable Name (14:15)

An interesting insight, touching on the contemporary Greek-Hebrew symbiosis of our book. Loss of a loved one, she reports, often occasioned the birth of a cult. The living were consoled, as the dead were raised to deific status, and

that one
who

a day ago
was only a corpse

is now
honored
as a god,

> and transmits
> to votaries
> initiations
> and sacrifices (14:15)

And the rulers intrude guiltily. To their advantage they encourage the rising of this or that cult. Access to heaven, intercessions, favor shed on an economy or a war—what king would not join, nay initiate, such pieties as attend the newly venerated!

> In time
>
> the practice
> gains strength,
>
> is fortified
> by law:
>
> graven images
> are worshipped
>
> by royal decree (14:16)

And a short step leads from royal endorsement of a new cult, to a cult of the royal personage himself. And this, be it noted, while the king abides in this mortal coil!

Thus the second source of idolatry mingles with the first,

> . . . and the masses,
> drawn
>
> by charming
> workmanship
> of an image,
>
> worshipped
> that one
>
> who
> shortly before
>
> they had honored
> as a man (14:20)

✦　✦　✦

That "charming workmanship" can be admired only with the gravest reservation: it is "a snare for humankind."

Are the Greeks caught in the snare? Are Hebrews as well endangered—and worse: some among them already fallen away, apostate?

Sophia knows it. God has spoken, sternly, unequivocally, to God's own:

You
shall not have

gods
other than Me.

You
shall not
carve

idols for yourselves,

in the shape
of anything
in the sky above

or the earth below

or the waters
beneath the earth.

You
shall not
bow down
or worship them (Exodus 20:3–5)

✦   ✦   ✦

14:22–31 A religion of politesse, a shady ecumenism—these are the unfit tools of distempered spirits, the accoutrements of apostates.

They have no hold on Sophia. The truth—let it be spoken. Lay the ax to root, and let the chips fall! Still, despite the loss and falling away, God

love(s)
the creation,

loathe(s)
nothing
that was made.

And again, the sublime logic:

For

what You hated,

You
would not have fashioned . . .

And yet again, insistent and consistent, both:

You
spare
all things
because

they are Yours,

O Lord
and Lover
of life.

✦   ✦   ✦

Abruptly, sweetness, and large-heartedness vanish. Transfigured Sophia stands there, in wild condemnation of Greek idolatries. A Woman of contrasts, on fertile ground she sows seeds far and wide.

(Paul will harvest the theme, in his diatribe against pagan idolatries and misconduct.)

Her analysis of unfaith, apostasy, and consequence is devastating. A phoenix eye ranges our tormented world—

Soon

it did not suffice
to err
in knowledge of God:

in the immense struggle
in which ignorance
plunged their lives

they call such evils—

"peace"! (14:22)

Ignorance brings in its wake a behavior ethically degraded, casting further darkness upon the mind. A hellish cycle is underway.

And that "immense struggle"—it rages too close for comfort. Within, without, in the soul, in public. The empery lays its claim, like a mailed hand on failed lives.

The conclusion, a twist of the blade:

They confer
on such evils

the name
"peace"!

✦   ✦   ✦

To a faithful Hebrew, the impoverishment—worse, the degradation— of the word *shalom* would be scarcely bearable. (The cognate verb implies completion, perfection: a human scheme of things in favor of humans. One striking parallel: "a debt paid".)

Precisely, the good life shines forth in holy ancestors and prophets. In the moral climate they create, ennoblement and mutuality are the norm. In their aura and example, "it is easy to be virtuous" (Peter Maurin).

✦   ✦   ✦

Shalom, the greeting, invoked God's blessing on the one encountered. What most mattered in life was there for the taking, available, a gift: from God, from and to one another. "Yahweh is peace" was the title of Gideon's altar (Judges 6:24). Shalom implies access, communion with the Deity, and in consequence godly behavior. Something of this: I dwell in God's peace, therefore I live and act for others.

✦   ✦   ✦

And we note too, the dark obverse of the *shalom* of God. Jeremiah sweated under its yoke, deriding the prostitution of a supreme good (6:14). Prophets of fat living cried "Peace, peace—and there was no peace." There was only the vile prospering of a few, a yoke of iron laid on the powerless.

He was blunt, this suffering servant, blunt as Sophia. No justice, no shalom.

✦   ✦   ✦

And wars and rumors of war: an infernal series of curses lies heavy on the quick and the dead. And on the unborn. No shalom, only blood vengeance, a curse.

A hideous example. In the time of Solomon, a general of the armies, Joab, turned against the king. His perfidy was discovered, he fled to a sanctuary. The news was brought to Solomon, himself hardly to be thought guiltless of bloodshed. The king speaks:

> Strike him down and bury him, and you will remove from me and from my family the blood which Joab shed . . .

> God will hold him responsible for his own blood, because he struck down two men better and more just than himself . . .

> Let their blood fall on the head of Joab and his descendants forever.

> But may David and his posterity and his dynasty and his throne know forever the shalom of Yahveh . . .(1 Kings 2:31–33)

"Know forever, shalom?" No shalom, but a curse.

The king proceeds to utter a prayer: specious, one thinks, and

impossible of granting to a "man of blood," Solomon—or for that matter
to his son David, or their clan.

How indeed one thinks, shall their god, a deity mirroring their warlike
image—how could Mars confer shalom? Oxymoronic, if not downright
demented, he thought.

✦   ✦   ✦

The same gift is central to the Christian bible: *eirene* for *shalom*. Peace
is the gift of Jesus to His disciples:

> Shalom
>
> is my farewell
> to you.
>
> I
> give it to you
>
> not
> as the world
> gives (John 14:27)

Shalom was a gift of parting. It is the gift of return:

> On the evening
>
> of that first day
> of the week . . .
>
> Jesus came
> and stood before them.
>
> "Shalom,"
> he said (John 20:19)

Shall others confer shalom? shall this world? The answer is an abrupt
rejection of absurdity, of a metaphysical impossibility. So by implication,
Paul declares:

> Then
> God's own peace,
>
> which is beyond
> all understanding,
>
> stand guard
> over your hearts and minds,
>
> in Christ Jesus (Colossians 4:7)

✦   ✦   ✦

Eirene is beyond the scope or power of this world, as shalom was beyond the power or scope of the god of Solomon. The two principalities, "world" and "god" being closely related signs of turmoil, moral chaos, the Fall.

How is the world to confer eirene or shalom, "the world" being busied, in its acolytes and structures—on conflict, chaos, vagary, treachery, ethical squalor, demagoguery, mendacity, unappeased choler, mass murder?

No, another source must be invoked, the Mystery, our vocation, the cherishing of unity.

The imperative signals an utmost urgency:

> Christ's peace
> must reign
> in your hearts,
>
> since
> as members
> of the one Body,
>
> you have been called
> to that peace (Colossians 3:15)

✦   ✦   ✦

Sophia's indictment rages on, a diatribe reminiscent of Paul, a catalog of utmost wickedness.

Then this (verse 27), by way of summary:

> The cult
> of nameless idols
>
> is the essence,
> source,
>
> and extreme form
> of all evil.

✦   ✦   ✦

Abrupt, and yet how rich in implication. The idols are "nameless," which is to say, they have no proper existence. Or another turn is suggested: naming the idols is forbidden.

Thus among the Greeks, the Erinyes were "named" the "nameless ones." Beware them. For in a name conferred or spoken lurks power:

> Never
>
> mention
> the name

of another god.

It
shall not
be heard
from your lips (Exodus 23:13)

Such warnings, given the darkness of the hour—of the present hour—could only be regarded as salutary.

✦ ✦ ✦

Shocking Sophia: a double crime is adduced:

Idolaters
have made
of God
a false idea.

Wicked,
they have sworn

contrary
to the truth (14:30)

It would seem plausible that the "double crime" is in reality one. Two aspects are suggested. Affirming idols subverts the truth: the truth that God is God, that the "unnamed others" are not.

The subversion is also a perversion. Existence is stood on its head. In the mad logic of idolatry, the Existant One exists not, is a "false idea."

God is dethroned. From Reality itself to—"idea": and a false idea at that.

In support of the abomination, an oath is sworn. The oath is implied in the will to bend the knee, to offer fealty before "stocks and stones."

✦ ✦ ✦

If God is reduced to a nothing—and worse, to a "false idea"—a question arises, inevitably. What then, or who, is to be acknowledged as true, and more than an "idea"—a reality?

And more—who is Reality Itself?

Who is supreme, who to be adored?

Who sets moral limits (or dissolves them)?

What new Deuteronomy is to be promulgated, from what high mountain, and by whom?

What personal and public behaviors are commended? what forbidden? Who is (are) to announce in the world, eminence, governance? Who to reward and chastise?

✦ ✦ ✦

To the first question. According to the reprobates, the nameless, lifeless "works of our hands," these—are—reality. These perform the functions mentioned, these are granted divine prerogatives.

And the order of existence is reversed. True God is thereby denied a capital letter. On the gods is conferred one.

✦ ✦ ✦

15:1–3 Sophia, and another astonishing change of mood. She urges a new tack, a reminder. Let us suppose that renegades and their idols are disposed of, that the truth is in the air.

Now the author of Wisdom speaks in the name of Her own, the faithful ones. In that sublime guise, bound to truth as though wound about in phylacteries, let him address a prayer to true God. To Herself.

And She will give ear.

The prayer implies a bracing warmth of spirit. It is as though the people in diaspora were transported home. They stand once more in the temple. Those who pray are of the household of the faith, and know it. Thus a swift change of tone.

The awful "it," the nameless ones, those who can only be spoken about, who are lifeless "stocks and stones"—that dire revelation yields sweetly—to a "Thou."

It is Her votaries who raise the prayer. Fittingly, in Her honor they borrow the immemorial phrases of the prophets:

> Good You are,
> and how truthful!
>
> Slow
> to anger,
>
> mercifully
> You govern all . . . (15:1)

Thus a fair beginning. Knowing Sophia, knowing as well the pretension and predation of the gods, the people are steeped in a saving self-knowledge.

Some among them, to the chagrin and loss of the faithful, have fallen away, beckoned by the lure of the idols. Their sedition dramatizes once more the venomous power of the Fall: it is

> reason
> and source
> and extremity
>
> of all evil (15:4)

The truth is dire, the danger near. If some have apostatized, all are vulnerable. For fidelity to the truth is beyond human power: it is a gift of Sophia to Her own.

Confess then, you who waver and turn and turn about. Confess need of Sophia, confess sinfulness, confess longing for relief from sin.

And above and beyond all—confess to the fidelity of holy Sophia:

> Even
> if we sin,
>
> we remain
> Yours,
> knowing
> Your power.
>
> But
> we will not sin,
> knowing
> we are Yours (15:2)

Let us dare, let us put the matter flatly. Sophia would have it so: has She not instructed us?

> To know You well
>
> is
> perfect justice (15:3)

That "knowing" draws You to our side, draws life-giving grace into soul and body. Through Your love, we look on the world and time and sin and death—as well as those ever so faint hints of glory-be—we look on all things with Your eyes, Sophia.

And that "justice" of yours—that abused, abandoned, holy waif, lost in the wilderness of the Fall! You, Sophia, mother of all, rescue the child, take him in Your arms, succor and restore the one born of You: Justice!

He turns his sweet face to us. And we are lost in wonder: how he resembles You! And how could it be otherwise, since he is the fruit of Your womb, Your favorite child.

✦ ✦ ✦

See, You pass him, the Just One, into our arms, our lives. Now he is our charge in the world: we, the honored godparents of Justice. Ours to protect and shield and cherish this endangered One, whom the principalities of this world detest, even to this extreme of malice, "seeking the life of the child."

Knowing the child Justice, looking in his eyes, doing his works in the world—thus we know You, Sophia

✦   ✦   ✦

Your might

is the root
of immortality (15:3)

Sophia has already stated as much. Dramatically, She has told the
story of Her favorites, the "poor and just ones," who through the ages
have fallen prey to persecution and death.

The lives and deaths of these holy victims she has recounted in loving
detail:

If
before others

they seemed
punished,

yet their hope
brims

with immortality (3:1–9)

In the eyes of Wisdom, their story is an absolute conquest of vocation
over blind fate. The victims become the victors, the protagonists of true
memory, honored in the heroic behavior of those who come after, in the
pages of holy bible, in liturgies summoning their intercession.

And what of the victimizers? They stand under a stark judgment:

Neglecting justice,
abandoning the Lord,

the wicked
shall receive

a chastisement
to match their thoughts.

They who despise wisdom and instruction
are doomed:

vain is their hope,
fruitless their labors,
worthless their works (3:10–11)

15:4–6 The prayer takes a dark turn. The obverse of fidelity is summoned, shadowy and haunting—schism. Some have bowed before "strange
gods before Me." Sadder they are than a Pygmalion, who fell in love with
the statue he had created.

Such deviations are described in contemptuous detail, even as they are
renounced in a kind of negative Credo:

The fabrications
of perverse art

have not led us
astray.

nor
sterile daubs

smeared
with wild colors—

those spectacles
arouse

the passion
of manifest fools,

longing
to embrace

the inanimate form
of a dead image (15:4–5)

The images deceive, even as with perverse power, they draw to themselves

those
who make them

and long for them and worship them (15:6)

As though She declared: "Enough said."

✦   ✦   ✦

15:7–10 Well, not quite enough. Another dose of contempt is offered a like folly: Sophia takes a close look at the potters—these worthies fill the market stalls with their cheap clay gods.

Scornful Sophia once more borrows the dramatic irony of Isaiah. In his parable, as we have seen, a craftsman of double mind uses creation both well and badly. And he is sublimely ignorant of the difference.

Thus too, this potter:

Laboriously
working the soft earth,

he molds
serviceable vessels—

and then
their opposite,

> each and all
> jumbled
> together (15:7)

Such "innocence" is perverse, money driven. The artisan must be summoned to account. How dare he assert or imply that

> What
> shall be
> the use of each,
>
> he alone
> is to judge (15:7)

What is the office of Sophia here, what will serve to awaken the sleepwalkers? Shall She mime them at work, caricature their labors in a stinging rebuke?

She will. For a start she offers a metaphor and a biblical truth. Potters work in clay, that genetic substance. And of clay the potter himself has been created.

> Does he not know that in a short
> yesterday
>
> he was drawn forth
> from the earth.
>
> Let him grow wise. All too
>
> shortly,
> he will return
>
> to the clay
>
> from which
> he was drawn (15:8)

Does the clay in his hands not tell him this, that his span of life briefly draws him forth, only to return him, melded, unrecognizable, back to the same earth?

And more, is he ignorant that a life worth living is laced with accountability? How can it be, that

> with misspent toil
>
> and from
> the same clay,
>
> he molds
> a meaningless god? (15:9)

✦   ✦   ✦

Could folly go further? In the eyes of Sophia, indeed it could. This crude-handed artisan, all thumbs! He is demented: he thinks to rival the great artists of Greece, "goldsmiths and silversmiths and molders of bronze," whose art is honored and envied throughout the world. An appalling adventurer, he sets to work—on counterfeits. And the outcome?

> Ashes
> his heart is.
>
> More worthless
> than dirt
>
> is his hope,
>
> more ignoble
> than clay
>
> his life (15:10)

And the reason, the source of this falling away from good sense?

> Because
> he knew not
>
> the One
> who fashioned him,
>
> breathed
> into him
> a quickening soul,
>
> infused
> a vital spirit (15:11)

15:12–13 Truth told, such a one wanders the adult world, a perpetual child. He plays a game for vile profit, while issues of life and death pass him by, mindless, frivolous as he is.

To Sophia, the performance is outrageous. It is "our life" which is at stake, that precious gift from on high, "our existence." For a coin in the palm, community is huckstered, frittered away, life itself cheapened to a commodity.

Such a one, conceding nothing to the neighbor, offering nothing, is a kind of ethical amputee.

Thus Sophia, innocence Itself, reads the hearts of humans. In the soul of the idol maker, incised in stone she discovers a text both cynical and cramped:

> One
> must profit
>
> by
> whatever means—
>
> be they evil (15:12)

But does such a one not know that the means are in the end, the end in the means? In his work both are vitiated beyond recognition. Money for idols, idols for money. We have a falling away from the truth of life, an ancient treachery—and a contemporary.

✦ ✦ ✦

The Isaian parallel is striking. Has the Fall been dramatized with greater skill? An artisan sets to work. His soul is divided: it is as though right and left hand were strangers, as they move utterly at cross purpose:

> (He) . . . lays hold of . . . trees of the forest, which God has planted and the rain made grow, to serve for fuel.
>
> With a part of their wood he warms himself, or makes a fire for baking bread.
>
> But with another part he makes a god, which he adores, an idol which he worships.
>
> Half of it he burns in the fire, and on its embers he roasts his meat . . .
>
> Of what remains he makes a god, his idol, and prostrate before it in worship, he implores it: "Rescue me, for you are my god" (Isaiah 44:14–17)

✦ ✦ ✦

15:14–19 Egypt, and its befouled animal-gods, what a bitter memory! Sophia gives it full play. The oppressor churned out a wide array of idols. Not content with these, the Egyptians indulged in a perverse ecumenism. They seized on the gods of the surrounding nations, and made them their own.

Another contemptible aspect of such behavior. The maker of idols, despite his duped greed, remains nobler than his artifact.

At least, the artisan is living:

> No one
> succeeds
> in fashioning
>
> a god
> likened
> to himself:
>
> mortal,
> he makes
>
> with impious hands
> a dead thing (15:16–17)

✦ ✦ ✦

These people! One might think that in choosing fauna for veneration, they would seek out the nobler beasts. No such thing:

> Nothing
> of beauty,
> nothing attractive—
>
> but
> such beasts
>
> as lack
> approval
> or blessing (15:19)

✦ ✦ ✦

And finally, an extended midrash, a rabbinical reworking of earlier stories. Much of the material undergoes a sea change, into something wonderful and strange. Indeed.

Israelites and Egyptians are subject to parallel treatment: parallel, but harshly contrasting. The former are condignly punished. The beasts whose favors they sought turned ferocious tooth and claw against them.

And what of the Israelites, their failings, their fate before the Deity? These are another matter entirely.

✦   ✦   ✦

Would this overstate the case? In these concluding chapters, the Israelites simply could do no wrong. Late Jewish literature is embedded here. And it flies in the face of Exodus and Numbers.

As memories recede, harsh lines soften. Earlier it was asserted time and again that the Israelites sinned. They "murmured" against God and Moses. In the absence of the seer, Aaron was inveigled to cast an idol, a calf of gold. Then they fell in worship before the pitiful talisman.

More. On occasion the authority of Moses rankled and roiled. The people broke into rebellion, and were punished horrifically.

And so on, a catalog of mordant arrogance, a dark cycle of crime and punishment.

✦   ✦   ✦

To the rabbis, all this is intolerable. They bring a far different sensibility to events, softening the ills that issue in a firestorm from the pages of the earlier books.

Strong in the later temperament, overriding all else, is a sense of the providential love that governs this people. All deviance admitted, not a scintilla of divine love is withdrawn: they remain the "chosen."

And if it be true (and it is so attested through the ages) that covenant creates and sustains a sense of walking steady in a shaky world—then on these latter pages, sin shall perennially be denied pride of place. Forgiveness, prevenient love before all!

So a daringly different version of events rises to the surface of common consciousness. Darkness be banished! (or nearly so).

✦   ✦   ✦

And again, an implication. Let the faithful, generation after generation, judge between the former chroniclers and the rabbinical scholars.

Which version, whose bias and moral summing up, seize upon heart and mind, awaken and sustain hope? Which account is truer to human capacity for goodness? Which is truer to the truth of covenant?

We choose, we judge—even as we are judged.

Mercy, Compassion are God's other Names—uttered, taught, insisted on by God's oracles, the prophets. And with regard to the enslaving goys, the Egyptians, a dark brow and a darker intent turns away from them. Other Names of the Deity are dredged up: the Judge, the implacable One, the Author of plagues.

chapter nine

"A plague of storms for the idolatrous, a rain of manna for the faithful" (16:1–29)

16:1–4 The perduring dualism starts here.

Let us assume that, for strong reason, other intentions, ideologies, interests have shouldered into the text. Sophia has yielded to a frosty rabbinical eye. The mood of suavity and tenderness undergoes a striking, even shocking change.

To our comfort and strengthening, the spirit of Sophia lay tenderly on the text—for awhile. Now the generous protocol vanishes. Once more (and how wearyingly), firm boundaries are set in place: the chosen versus the outsiders.

And the god? He is male, and a stern dualistic sensibility rules the text—he has provided a diet of delight for the chosen, and a repulsive vomit-inducing victual for the foe.

Rabbinical intent and method are clear: we have seen them at work before. Recall the ancient tale, ply it anew. Soften or harden the circumstance of friend and enemy. Bring the god into the action in ways that underscore preference and despise, virtue and reward, crime and punishment.

An example. The Israelites demand delectable meats, but no default is imputed, no punishment befalls.

Then a parallel, contrasting ethos: a harsh implication (altogether absent in the original) is drawn from the episode of the plague of frogs: hunger forces the Egyptians to consume the repulsive beasties that so afflict them.

Talk about a midrash!

✦ ✦ ✦

16:5–7 Another remarkable turn. In the original, we are told of divine outrage, as a detestable "murmuring" breaks out, challenging the deity and his subaltern Moses.

"In punishment" burning serpents are dispatched among the people. Multitudes perish.

Moses is instructed thereupon to mold a bronze serpent and mount the image on a pole. Let the afflicted ones gaze on the serpent, and they will be healed. We have here a typical pattern in Exodus-Numbers: sin-consequence-mitigation.

✦   ✦   ✦

Now for the contrast. With will and skill, the rabbinical tale alters the earlier version. Thus: "briefly," a "reprimand" was issued against the community.

What form did the reproof take? We are not told. Only that the people had a "sign of salvation" available: it "recalled to their minds the precepts of the law."

Thus, a substantial correction of the original:

> The one
> who turned
> toward the serpent
>
> was saved
> not
> by what he saw,
>
> but by You,
>
> Savior of all (16:7)

✦   ✦   ✦

At a stroke, the revisionists remove from the symbol any trace of syncretism or magic. The afflicted gaze on the bronze serpent, but the image is denied all healing power: they are saved by Another.

✦   ✦   ✦

A further recalling and correcting of the episode: in this one, Jesus speaks:

> Just as Moses
> lifted up
>
> the serpent
> in the desert—
>
> so must
> the Human One
> be lifted up,
>
> that in Him
>
> all
> who believe
> may have eternal life (John 3:14–17)

Thus a triple "lifting up" of the Human One—in death, in new life, in glory unending.

And we are summoned to "look upon" this Event, this hard wood of shame and glory, this crux of all, the pivot of time and creation—the cross and its Burden, first plunged in our soil, then set free and weightless, living and borne above.

The Healing One. And the open eye of faith—what does it see? The truth, the cost, the consequence. We gaze, we accept the awesome implication for those who would be accounted human, faithful. That Reality, so abused, so trammeled: the cost, the consequence.

And so gazing, so following through, we are made safe. The fangs of Old Wily leave us untouched.

✦   ✦   ✦

16:8–12 Another daring recapitulation.

For a start, once more we have a supposition unverified in Exodus. "Our enemies" have been informed that the god "delivers from all evil." Delivers "all," that is, except "the enemy."

Such knowledge must be thought to widen the breach set against amity: some are saved, others not. "The enemies" are fated to perish under the bites of "locusts and flies."

This too goes unmentioned by the author of Exodus.

✦   ✦   ✦

We are in wonderment. Are the authors not contradicting themselves? Have they not, shortly before, invoked a "universal Savior"? And does not such a God cancel all prior enmities and ruinous dualisms, in love for all?

As for the poisonous snakes, a far different outcome befalls the chosen. Even they, it would seem, require from time to time a reminder of Your injunctions.

In the desert years, the call to remembrance came in this inauspicious, often fatal form: venomous stings. Fatal, but not to those under a special providence:

> swiftly
> they were healed (16:11)

And as to the source of healing, let it be made clear:

> Neither
> herb nor ointment
> cured them,
>
> but
> Your all healing word . . . (16:12)

✦ ✦ ✦

16:13–14 And yet another vigorous submission before a superhuman power. This god, as the author confesses, holds dominion over life and death. His power is absolutely uncontained by circumstance: even at the gate of Sheol, the god can summon the dead back to life. Such power is in sharp contrast to the relative powerlessness of humans:

> Humans
>
> slay
> in malice . . .
>
> they cannot
> summon back
>
> the soul
>
> Hades
> has received
> for its own (16:14)

The sentiments are disturbingly accurate. "Humans slay in malice." Indeed we do, year upon year, eon upon eon.

Still, one cannot but recall this revision of history, set down with a kind of pious savoring of a lethal scene:

> The sting
> of locusts and flies
> slew them
>
> and
> no remedy
> was at hand . . . (16:9)

Is the god then, to be thought devoid of "malice"? Or for that matter, is the author himself free of such? With approval, even with a kind of awe, he enlarges an ungodly episode. The deity turns toward "the enemy." A dark look portends—no benignity is to follow.

And an entirely different gaze rests on the chosen. Punishment for the outsider, benefits heaped on the beloved.

✦ ✦ ✦

16:15–21 The manna is recalled, with a lyric enlarging of the legend:

> You
> nourished your own
>
> with
> the food
> of angels,

bread from heaven
ready to hand,
untoiled for,

endowed
with delight,

answering
every taste (16:20)

That cornucopia tipped, a veritable storm of beneficence! Impossible
to surrender the theme. Enlarge it then, savor it:

this
substance of yours,

revealing
your sweetness
toward your own,

pleasing
the tongue of each,

blended
to whatever flavor . . . (16:21)

chapter ten

"Darkness afflicts Egypt, but a flaming pillar guides on the unknown way" (17:1–18:4)

17:1–14 A veritable apogee of midrash! All sources are drawn upon: biblical accounts (sedulously corrected to be sure), Jewish legends, rabbinic speculation. And of no less moment, images and reflections original to the author.

Greek influences as well? Indeed, distinguished footprints cross the text: the rather pretentious "fine writing" of verses 10–12 and the search for causality of verses 10–12. One could add as well, the influence of a number of Greek legends enshrined in writings known as "Descents into Hell."

For instance, it is told in Exodus that darkness descended suddenly on the Egyptians. The account is straightforward, all but telegrammed:

> Moses stretched out his hand toward the sky
> and for three days, there was intense darkness
> throughout the land of Egypt.
>
> Men could not see one another,
> nor, for three days,
> could they move from where they were (Exodus 10:22–23)

✦ ✦ ✦

Now for an immensely complex, cunning embroidery.

On some, we are told, the dark descended as they tarried at home. These, though safe under their roof, were hardly comforted. A horrendous nightmare followed, peopled by images of remorse and rent by fear:

> Even though
> no monstrous thing
> appeared,
>
> they shook
> at the passing
> of insects,
>
> the hissing
> of reptiles.

They
perished
trembling (17:9–10)

And so on and on. Has the art of midrash ever dared more than this full-rigged fantasy, launched and wildly set sailing?

Effortlessly our author skims o'er the bounding main.

But, but, the mind registers a caveat. Does he convey a fiction unverified elsewhere—that the plagues do not follow one on another, as Exodus would have it, but all clot together, in torment of the victims?

✦ ✦ ✦

17:15–21 And what of the fate of this or that Egyptian who perhaps was trapped in darkness, out of doors? Worse and worse befalls:

Wherever
he was,

he fell
confined
in an unbarred prison—

farmer, shepherd,
solitary workman—

taken unawares

they fell,

victims
of ineluctable necessity (17:16–17)

That "ineluctable necessity"—a neat Greek touch, summing things up.

✦ ✦ ✦

What to make of these somewhat bizarre inventions and inflations? Are they plausible, or campy, or polemical—or something of each?

Is the author perhaps dispatching a warning, a call to the Jewish renegades? Is a suggestion lodged here: that these are a species of new-age Egyptians, their apostasy hanging over them like palpable darkness?

✦ ✦ ✦

18:1–4 Exploration of the darkness-light theme continues. And a delicious, if minor midrash: while Egyptians are shrouded in darkness, Hebrews bathe in light.

And an interchange, logically beyond imagining:

The Egyptians
who heard voices
but did not see forms

(since now
they too suffered),

called (the Hebrews)
blessed.

And because
the formerly wronged
did no harm

they thanked them
and asked pardon . . . (18:1–2)

As usual, nothing of this is in the original. In one laconic sentence, we are simply told:

But the Israelites
had light
where they dwelt (Exodus 10:23)

chapter eleven

"Death to the Egyptian firstborn; the Hebrew children are saved" (18:5–19:22)

18:5–13 What derring-do!

Yet another new angle on the ancient tale. Here, a connection is contrived: pharaoh's decree of infanticide is linked with the plague that brought death to the first-born of Egypt.

Once more, any such connection is lacking in the original.

Throughout these closing chapters, as noted, such discrepancies abound. Each seems designed to place the virtue of the Israelites in a strong light, contrasted with the baffled obstinacy of the "enemy."

✦ ✦ ✦

Now and again (not often to be sure!), a ray of compassion gleams. At one point, stricken, the adversaries undergo a desolate change of heart:

Though . . .

on account of sorceries
they disbelieved,

at the death
of the first-born

they confessed:

"this people
was son of god!" (18:13)

✦ ✦ ✦

18:14–19 In the apocalyptic mode, our author pursues this highly tendentious revision.

Once for all, let disputed matters be clarified: god versus the gods, virtue versus perfidy, choice versus disowning. The rule: amplify, amplify! And always with a view to heightening the dualism, the conflict.

189

✦   ✦   ✦

Generations have passed since the original exodus. And the dead, alas, are forbidden rest. Odious memories are unsheathed like a gauntlet of swords.

Let us confess, it is all quite wearisome, this tedious tribalism, its awful persistence. To what point are such images—a regressive god and his fearsome tribe, winners and losers, light and darkness?

At least, one thinks, to this advantage. We are being shown—and urged to take warning—the dangers of misuse of memory.

Dangerous misuse. The dead are summoned to punish the living, and to be punished. Wrongs are recalled and dwelt on, pain is inflamed and swells in the telling.

Seemingly intent on revenge, a god long superceded by the God of Isaiah is summoned from the shades. We know him (sic) well.

Larger than life, the god broods over the historical books. He is champion of the killer-kings, more overbearing than a Goliath, a superhuman contrived by a Homer. For centuries he bestrode the world, knowing no challenge.

His was our only world: we were fallen from grace, and he our god.

Until the prophets. Then, along with his proud acolytes, the deity was unmasked, this god of power and might. Dethroned, he vanished, an emblem of human prehistory.

✦   ✦   ✦

Yet again here, he (sic) is summoned and rules the text, justifying war, decreeing the death of the innocent, vindicating the "insiders" who stand invincibly in the light.

Acculturated memory indeed, in service of ideology.

✦   ✦   ✦

Unsettlingly familiar is this fashioning of a god to our liking, our nationalism, tribalism, racism, wars. Let accusative records, if they touch on the honor of the chosen, be expunged. Let criminal episodes of ancestry be cleansed of fault. Rewrite, make it new, plausible—pandering.

And likewise, make sacred the story. Stamp it "God's word." Make of it the expression of the divine will.

Summon the god of the sword, the blade of extinction:

> . . . your all-powerful word
> bounded,
>
> a fierce warrior
> into the doomed land,

> bearing
> the sharp sword
> of inexorable decree.
>
> He alighted,
> filled every place
> with death . . . (18:15–16)

And more, along the same lines. This dangerous, omnivorous deity differs not at all from the god of the Egyptians.

✦ ✦ ✦

The text in sum, from chapter 11 forward, has been placed in other hands: Holy Sophia has vanished. Was She "too much with us," must she be stripped of credentials, in face of the aspirations of kings, kingmakers, and their necessary gods?

In any case, we note that her displacement is worked with considerable skill, gradually. In the beginning, in Egypt, She is celebrated as the mentor of great Moses, fueling his will to a flame of resistance.

But even then a line is being drawn: the "holy" against the "oppressors."

Can we envision the all but unbearable anomaly? Once Her hands were empty, welcoming, raised in blessing. But now a sword has appeared, drawn. Forgiveness, healing, those governors of holy behavior, recede. In their place ancient memories, grim and irksome, are summoned, ghosts from old graves:

> It was She
> who delivered
>
> the holy and blameless
> from the oppressors.
>
> She
> entered the soul
> of God's servant,
>
> withstood
> fearsome kings
>
> with signs and portents . . . (10:15–16)

Plagues, then mass killing in the Red Sea: gentle Sophia is transformed, a veritable Fury in the Greek image.

Or another image. The Heart and Soul of the earlier chapters has receded into the pantheon and been absorbed there.

Or yet another: Sophia, all tenderness and compassion, is turned to marble. She is a nameless caryatid, a pillar of the Realm of Necessity.

What, we marvel and mourn, has become of the praise of universal love that earlier rose in healing fragrance from her lips?

> For
>
> You love
> all things
> that exist
>
> and detest
>
> none of the things
> You have made.
>
> You
>
> would not
> have made anything
> if You hated . . .
>
> You
> spare all things
> for they are Yours,
>
> Lord and Lover of souls . . . (11:24–26)

✦ ✦ ✦

And what "instruction" for ourselves, lurks in this sea change of tone and office?

The prophets are sure guides in a vexing matter. They urge us to acknowledge an edgy truth. In such a world as ours, the knowledge of God, the God of Jesus, is indeed precarious. National histories, constantly in ferment, ridden with self-serving myth, favor an ancestry presided over not by the Spirit of Sophia but by the old gods of war and greed and pride of place. Haul them out then, set them in place, bow, pay fealty!

How difficult, how lonely the way of Jesus, of holy Sophia, edged as they are out of imperial history, declared irrelevant, useless as a font of conduct, a "way."

✦ ✦ ✦

"For the duration" of whatever war, the gospel is replaced by a military handbook and in effect, Jesus is exiled.

More, the decree of exile is often legitimated by a species of court prophets and their just war fantasies—ideologues, Christian ethicists, White House counselors, televangelists—and a former notorious cardinal of New Work. Their message is alike: "My country right or wrong, but my country."

Thus a dark "fifth gospel," issuing blessings on imperial self-interest, nudges our testament aside.

✦ ✦ ✦

18:20-25 Talk about hyperbole in the service of history!

The tactic must work to advantage in two directions, as we have seen.

Syncrisis therefore: exaggerate or mitigate as required. As to the first, the enemy must not only perish, he must know to his last breath remorse and despair multiplied.

✦ ✦ ✦

And a further problem arises, as we have seen. According to the older chronicles, the "holy nation," the "chosen," have offended grievously in the wilderness. The episodes are stark, extended in the telling, dire in consequence.

How deal with these? Mitigate, tell of repentance, admission of default, damage minimized.

Let it be clear that the "chosen" do not fall from grace. They fall, yes, vaguely out of favor. They fall into guilt. And yes, granted: multitudes are hurled into Sheol, into death.

And yet, and yet. Living or dead they remain the "just." Even under condign punishment, their status before the god is presented as immeasurably superior to that of the "enemy."

Paradoxes aplenty, if not contradictions.

Paradoxes, one thinks, also illumining the current situation, our own:

At one time
death

touched
even the just . . .
Yet
not for long
did anger last.

For
the blameless one

hastened
to champion them . . . (18:20-21)

✦ ✦ ✦

In a bitter hour, the dualistic duel is interrupted. A "champion," Aaron, stops the carnage short by

the weapon
of his special office,

prayer
and propitiating incense.

And

on his full-length robe

was
the whole world. . . .

He intercedes for all.
Even for Egyptians?

✦   ✦   ✦

An image suggests itself: two streams, side by side, uneasy flowing.

Correction. One stream only, let us say, of chosen and goys.

And yet the image fails: the history can hardly be termed a stream at all. It is stilled, a tarn metaphysically frozen in place.

The image aptly symbolizes the just: though these be taken in crime and grievously punished, they can never be termed unjust.

Let a like image symbolize the goys. They too are frozen in place. Pereant! Let them perish.

They are stigmatized forever: the "enemy."

✦   ✦   ✦

Yet another image: a stream. It flows through time, gently as "sweet Avon": its waters are cleansing, reconciling, forgiving. This is the Mosaic stream, the Isaian. The stream named Jesus. It heals the entire creation. Against monstrous odds, its healing has reached even—ourselves.

✦   ✦   ✦

19:1–13 To the conclusion of our fiercely corrected (and contested) Exodus.

Shall one summon an extended poetic license?

Only imagine: across the great divide of the sea, lovingly it seems and in awe, passes first the vanguard, then the entire tribe, the chosen. Impetuous waves part. Where only dense waters were, dry land appears.

Was not great Moses himself moved at the miracle to utter a paean? Let the chosen too wax poetic, ecstatic, recalling this (verse 6) very Greek "reconstitution" of nature:

Creation

with all its elements,
was refashioned

in subservience
to Your commands

so that Your servants
might be preserved

unscathed.

And among the miracles wrought for the faithful, the parting of the
waters was hardly to be accounted the first:

They gazed
at the cloud

overshadowing
the camp . . .

at an open road
out of the Red Sea . . .

across which
the nation passed

under the shelter
of Your hand,

after all the marvels
they had seen . . .

Wonder upon wonder! After ferocious pain, they witnessed so great an
epiphany and were transported with joy:

Like
horses in pasture

they ranged free,

bounding about
like lambs,

praising you
O god,

their deliverer.

✦   ✦   ✦

Then, O then. As to the unchosen, what of them?

in mourning rites

they adopted
another
senseless plan:

those
they
had begged to depart,

they
then pursued as fugitives . . . (19:3)

In the author, a kind of unholy glee erupts. Bitter memory offers a cold comfort, ancient scores are being paid:

Compulsion
drew them on . . .

amnesiac
they were.

So
they completed

the full measure
of torment . . .

and found
an unheard-of ending (19:4)

✦   ✦   ✦

19:14–22 Imagine, the Egyptians are ethically worse than Sodomites! The ancient renegades refused to honor visiting angels:

but these
reduced
to slavery

guests

who had performed
many a good work! (19:14)

No wonder then, the Egyptians were in effect stricken with blindness, as darkness enveloped the land.

✦   ✦   ✦

The tale is passed hand to hand like an ancient coin, generation to generation. And to what end?

We arrive at an utterly hopeful conclusion, encouraging the Jews of Alexandria amid their uneasy sojourn.

This God of Greek and Hebrew, God of the golden mean, God of Moses is also the One named Sophia, a Deity of truly seismic accommodation.

Astringent, audacious, invincible, surpassing and surprising, both.

Uneasy joining of oppositions, contradictions. Instructing, admonishing, reproving—*eccolo*, God has given glory to God!

> In every way
> You
>
> magnified
> Your people,
>
> unfailing
>
> You
> stood by them
>
> in every time
> and circumstance (19:22)